Pregnancy & M

An Honest and F

MW01235305

(and Anxiety, Sleeplessness and Total Life-Disrupting Insanity)

of Having a Baby

By:

Amanda Lattavo Berkeley
with
Kimberly Falen

Pregnancy & Motherhood: A Survival Guide.

An Honest and Fun Introspective on the Miracle *(and Anxiety, Sleeplessness and Total Life-Disrupting Insanity)* of Having a Baby

ISBN 978-1-505374-15-5
Published by CreateSpace
http://2mamabears.com
Acknowledgement
First and foremost, thank you to our husbands, who pushed and prodded us to write this book and who endured more than a few evenings of being ignored as we completed it!

To our daughters, who are our inspiration and from whom we draw our daily inspiration (and frustration) we love you more than life itself. T'iamo, we love you to the moon and back.

To Jessica Valentine, our mentor and publishing guru who stuck with us in the two years, and two additional pregnancies, it took us to complete this work!

Prelude – This book is not intended to be the end-all medical guide to your pregnancy or baby, nor is our intention to "tell" you what to do. We're giving you some basic advice that falls in line with the American Pregnancy Organization and American Academy of Pediatrics but more importantly, we're giving you an honest and funny look at pregnancy, labor, delivery and motherhood from the perspective of two career moms trying to keep our hair from falling out. We're going to provide some pages of references for more information and we're writing from more of a general perspective rather than trying to address every possible situation. And always, always, consult your doctor or pediatrician if you are ever unsure of anything!

We're so excited you're embarking on the crazy train of motherhood and we wanted to share what has (and has not) worked for us, assure that you can actually balance motherhood with your career, community involvement, keeping your house from being run over by rodents (aka housekeeping) and circle of friends – oh and keep your marriage hot as well. If you like our sense of humor and down to earth approach, please join the Facebook Group "2MamaBears" at https://www.facebook.com/pages/2MamaBears/850314454998902 for other moms' perspectives as well as updates from our blog, http://2mamabears.com

If you are easily offended, do not have a sense of humor or think that making fun of the miracle of life and joy that is motherhood is sacrilegious, then this probably is not the book for you!

The Authors

Amanda Lattavo Berkeley lives in Ohio with her partner-in-crime husband Doug and their two daughters, Samantha & Emma.

Kimberly Falen lives in Ohio with her ever-patient husband Mike and their three daughters, Allyssa, Addalyn & Aubree.

TABLE OF CONTENTS

Chapter 1 – Pregnancy – For Real

Ok, you peed on the stick and the result is positive. Now what? After you are done crying, laughing, sweating, and freaking out…take a deep breath. You are embarking on the single most joyous journey of your life: parenthood! And if you've been on the TTC (Trying To Conceive) bandwagon for awhile, the stress of getting pregnant and that TWW (Two Week Wait) hell-ride is behind you! Way to go! You got a sperm to connect to your egg! Woot! Woot!

After you have collected yourself (we know, your hormones are **already** raging), you need to decide who you will share your news with and when. Many people decide to share right away and others decide to wait until they have made it past the first trimester when the likelihood of miscarriage greatly decreases. For many women, your baby bump will not appear for several months, so keeping the news a secret from a physical perspective (unless you're projectile vomiting) is not usually difficult. The hardest part about keeping your secret under wraps is that it's all you can think about! Most likely, you are going to be smiling A LOT as you think about your baby 24/7.

That leads to our next point: you may hear other moms refer to something called "mommy brain." Please prepare yourself, this is real. During pregnancy and after the baby is born, your mind will be so filled with thoughts of your baby, you will likely experience any or all of the following: memory loss, forgetfulness, flakiness, and even airheaded-ness. Don't be alarmed, this is completely normal. You are becoming an absolute dipshit but it won't last forever. Women are so focused on every detail of their developing baby's life that it clouds their ability to think the way they did before pregnancy. The minute you see that positive sign, you are 24/7 every second of the day consumed with the baby, what's going on with your body, what size the growing dot is, risks, charts, countdowns, names, gender, nursery décor, maternity leave, boobs, dangers, hot flashes and 100 other things baby-centric. All day long. Especially when it's your first baby, it's ALL you can think about. When it's your second, third, fourth, you're still thinking about it, but you are focusing on so many other things / children that you aren't as fixated. So if this is your first baby – enjoy the fixation, brush up on the jargon and statistics and become a know it all. Because when your second comes along, there's no time for that stuff!

Along with your mommy brain, you can expect to experience a whole slew of crazy symptoms or none at all. We're going to go into that fun list here in a minute. Just be prepared, because one of the most entertaining aspects of being pregnant is hearing your doctor tell you, no matter your complaint, "It's your pregnancy." No really – doctors and nurses will attribute almost any ache, pain, sniffle, headache, hangnail or bruise to pregnancy. So when you hear other moms tell you the wild and wacky things they experienced during their pregnancy, don't laugh and think you're exempt. You're not! And if you happen to be one of those lucky ducks who has NO symptoms during your pregnancy, we don't like you a whole lot, but it's ok, because your baby still has to come out the same way and labor's a bitch no matter how you roll with it!

Some of the most common (this list is not all-inclusive!) symptoms of pregnancy:

Fatigue: We're not talking "gee, I'm a bit worn out" or "I'm a little sleepy," we're talking flat-out EXHAUSTION and it will hit you like the Roadrunner hitting a wall and knock you on your ass. We're talking about going to bed at 7 p.m. kind of exhaustion. It's a kind of wasted, life-sucking fatigue that you have never experienced before, unless maybe you've had Mono. The good news is, it goes away, generally, in your second trimester. As you enter the Second trimester, you perk up, you feel human and feel like you can be normal – take advantage and get the baby's room done, the baby registry done, and everything else done. Because fatigue comes back in the 3rd trimester and you're back to going to bed between 7 and 8 and will not be able to hold a conversation without yawning at least twice. Even at noon.

Nausea: This can range from "hmm I just don't feel quite right" to "holy shit just shoot me now!" Suggested remedies range from keeping some Saltines by your bed and eating a couple before you get up in the morning, keeping your diet light during the early months, Ginger chews, Ginger tea, wearing motion sickness bands, lozenges a.k.a. "baby pops," specifically for morning sickness (see a health food store or baby section of any major retailer), and eating more frequent, smaller meals so you don't get that empty feeling. Good luck!

Vomiting: There's an old wives' tale that says if you're throwing up, it means you have a healthy pregnancy and the baby is thriving. We'll go ahead and call bullshit on that because Kim never had any morning sickness with her first two girls and they're great! Amanda threw up weekly with her first, never with her second. For both our last pregnancies, daily nausea haunted us. It's just the way your body is processing all the changes in your hormones. Helpful Hint: keep the kitchen sink clear of dishes at all times. Sometimes the bathroom is just too far away!

Headaches: Hormones are to blame for almost every symptom you will have for the next 38 weeks and headaches are one of them. The good news is, by your 2nd trimester, your hormones level out and many of your pregnancy symptoms disappear. The bad news is, some symptoms never disappear until you get that child out of you! If you're a caffeine lady and trying to cut back or cut it out altogether, that will just exacerbate the problem. You can safely take acetaminophen products (think Tylenol) for what it's worth!

Sore Boobies: for some women, sore breasts are one of the first signs. For many husbands or partners, it is one of the downsides of pregnancy because it hurts to just have them breathed on, let alone touched!

Frequent Urination: also known as "oh my goodness I have to pee AGAIN?!" syndrome. Let me put it this way – you know how, when you're drinking, once you pee you've "broken the seal" and then all you do the rest of the night is pee every 20 minutes? Well, pregnancy breaks the seal and all you do is pee every 20 minutes. Well, maybe only on an hourly basis in the beginning, but definitely every 20 by your last month!

Lower Back Pain: there's a reason you see pregnancy women in their pregnant poses of hands behind their backs – their backs hurt! Even before you're carrying your bump, you may have that achy lower back that we usually only have with our periods. So really, being pregnant is sort of like being on your period for 40 weeks except you aren't bleeding – maybe. See the next symptom.

Sciatica: Not to be confused with lower back pain, we are talking about a pain that radiates (generally on one side of your body) from your hip down your leg and literally starts to impede your ability to walk. The baby starts to press on a muscle that puts pressure on the sciatic nerve that then causes you excruciating pain when you move. Try keeping yourself stretched with some yoga or pelvic tilts, massages and if it gets really awful, you may need to go to a chiropractor or neuromuscular therapist to try to get some relief. Unfortunately, the only real relief is birth.

Spotting: Yup, sometimes you spot. Now, there's a big difference between a little spotting or some old blood and LOTS of spotting bright red WITH cramps. By all means, call your doctor whenever you're concerned, but definitely call when you're cramping with bright blood. That could be a sign of something serious.

(Round) Ligament Pain: Your body has to prepare itself for what is about to happen – which is you growing a freaking basketball between your ovaries. Think about that for a minute – can you imagine how much stretching is about to occur between your hoo-ha and belly button? Well, you're going to feel it, because many women complain about ligament pain during the early months – it's where your uterus starts to stretch and get ready for the growing baby!

Food Cravings (or Aversions): We've all heard of women craving pickles and ice cream, or banana and marshmallow sandwiches, or protein, or sugar, or all of the above. There may also be foods that you absolutely love that become your enemy during pregnancy. For Amanda it was salad – any time she tried to eat salad, it would pay here back ten-fold with an upset stomach and a colon cleansing.

Bloating: Remember that period comment from before? Let's go ahead and add water retention to the list. In the early months, it may just be minor. In your later months, serious water retention could be a sign of something more serious – any weight gain of more than a couple pounds in a week isn't normal and could be a sign of pre-eclampsia. So as always, call your doctor if you think you're experiencing something not normal!

Pre-eclampsia: Since we've mentioned it, you also have a risk of gestational hypertension (high blood pressure due to pregnancy, which can cause headaches to you as well as an unusually high BP and stress on the baby) and the more serious pre-eclampsia. If you have high protein levels in your urine (tested during office visits), have high blood pressure consistently or if the baby starts to fail non-stress tests in the third trimester, you may be screened for pre-eclampsia or sent to the hospital for evaluation. Pre-eclampsia and gestational hypertension are both areas of concern for your baby and your doctor will keep a close eye on you to ensure both your and the baby's health. Amanda was induced three weeks early due to her gestational hypertension because of the risks to her youngest daughter. For more information, we'd like to direct you here: http://www.uptodate.com/contents/preeclampsia-beyond-the-basics

Acne: Remember how you used to have acne break-outs as a teenager? They're baaaack! Yup, this time, acne might pop up anywhere, in addition to skin tags and other skin problems. H-O-R-M-O-N-E-S. They're the devil.

Hair: Some hairdressers can tell you're pregnant just by the changes in your hair. You might experience thicker hair or greasier hair, or even some dandruff. You may also notice that when you wash your hair, you lose A LOT of it. Rest easy, you won't go bald and the ailments won't last forever. Just need to get those hormones out of your system.

Fingernails: Don't bother with those acrylics or shellac manicures right now – between your lovely hormones and the pre-natal vitamins you're taking daily like a good girl, your nails are kicking ass and taking names and growing too fast to keep up with the fills required for any special nail technology. Invest in clear coat ladies!

Nosebleeds: In addition to your expanding waistline, and joints and ligaments, your blood vessels are also expanding and maybe changing colors (see next symptom). Your body is pumping more blood to grow that bundle of joy, and as such, you're going to be more susceptible to bloody noses. In fact, your blood volume by the time you give birth will have increased anywhere from 20% to 40%! And we promise, you will in fact have a nosebleed hit at the most inopportune time, such as going into a meeting with your boss.

Blue Veins on your chest: (and elsewhere) – so you know that you're going to be pumping blood like a crazy woman. Well, sometimes those blood vessels turn blue in color because they're expanding and doing so much more work so they're more visible. Amanda started to look like the Smurfs had installed a racetrack on her chest from the veins on her chest from the armpits toher boobs.

Good stuff. They will go back to normal after pregnancy (unlike those pesky varicose veins you might get cursed with!)

Stuffy Nose: This is actually called rhinitis of pregnancy! Blame those hormones again! And chances are, if you weren't a snorer before pregnancy, you may become one. Get the snore strips – because sometimes you'll snore so loudly that you wake yourself up!

Mood Swings aka Psycho Mama: This is totally real and part of it is to blame on the hormones, the other part is welcome to the world of CONSTANT WORRY. Are you eating the right things? Are you allowed to take that vitamin? Is it possible to take too much Vitamin C for a cold (yes it is, actually). Is the baby developing at the right pace? Am I going to miscarry if (fill in the blank)? And that's with the baby not even HERE yet! All that worry, all the constant thinking about the baby will just make you crazy in addition to mommy's brain. Your partner needs to accept it and give you a pass because in addition to the worry and the hormones, you're also going to become the size of a cow and lose control of even the most basic bodily functions! See Sneeze Pee's.

Heartburn from Hell: This typically worsens as pregnancy progresses and the size of the belly starts to crowd the stomach, which forces acid into your esophagus. Also, let's hear it for hormones and that damn progesterone that's relaxing your muscles, including the stomach valve the keeps acid out of your esophagus. Ask your doctor if it gets really bad, because there are some OTC medications you can take to relieve some of the discomfort. Amanda and Kim both lived on heartburn pills.

Sneeze (or Laugh) Pee's: Start wearing panty liners now and buying stock in them, because between the cervical mucus (see below) and the gradual loosening of all things bladder related, you will inevitably get the sneeze pee's. People aren't kidding when they say practice your kegels! That will help, but there will still be at least one moment when you sneeze or god forbid laugh, and then next thing you know....you've pee'd your pants.

Passing Gas: You are about to become a champion farter. Get over it.

Cervical Mucus: You know that great stuff that signaled to you that you're ovulating (egg white mucus) and that you needed to make that baby? Well, just when you think it's disappeared as you anticipate your period, it's going to start coming back. And just get more and more plentiful. Really – invest in panty liners, because you're going to need them.

Sensitivity to Smells: So while you may crave (or hate) certain foods, you may find you develop the nose of a bloodhound and become very sensitive to certain smells. Like being able to tell that your colleague smoked a cigarette two days ago, or the smell of Subway is suddenly the most repulsive smell in the world (yup, Amanda was unable to go to Subway for 8 months).

Constipation: The discussion of poop starts before baby, because the doctor wants to make sure Mama is pooping regularly too. Sometimes you stay completely on schedule, sometimes you slow down a bit, and sometimes you just stop altogether. Talk to your doctor if you're having problems expelling daily or maybe every couple days. You want to stay regular!

The moment you share your pregnancy news, you are going to be bombarded with advice, opinions, and horror stories. For some reason, other moms feel the need to share their labor and delivery nightmares with newly pregnant women. It's like pregnancy and labor and delivery are the red badge of courage for women and when we hear someone is pregnant with their first, it's time to haze the new guy! It continues even after you've had the baby, as everyone will judge your child's behavior, appearance, etc... when you're anywhere so get used to it.

The best advice we can give you when it comes to filtering all that unsolicited advice, is to take it in, filter it, and then decide if it is anything you want to use. From this moment on, you need to do what works best for you and your new family. The advice can become so overwhelming, and annoying, that we actually have a whole chapter devoted to it because pregnancy is just the tip of the iceberg. There are some things you want to think about early into your pregnancy. Is your gynecologist also an obstetrician (OB/GYN)? If not, it is a good idea to start shopping for one, unless you plan to keep your bun in the oven eternally. You need a medical professional who can deliver your baby, not just keep your tunnel of love and ovaries healthy. They will also be able to provide all the necessary medical information you need regarding: diet, health risks, items of concern, exercise, safety, etc. You may also want to start thinking about your options for childcare after baby is born. If are lucky enough to stay home with your babes, problem solved! If not, hit the daycare circuit fast because some places (even nannies and in-home childcare) have significant waiting lists.

You and your partner also need to talk about and prepare for your labor and delivery. A lot of women decide to create a birth plan along with their partner and medical professional. That's great! But, please understand there are a million scenarios that can happen between the time you pee on the stick and the time you are holding that precious baby in your arms. We can't stress enough, that while it's great to have a birthing plan, you have to also accept that deviations from that plan may become necessary and that's OK! All you want is that baby out of you and in your arms – method of delivery isn't nearly as important as healthy baby in your arms. Down the road, in your third trimester, you may also want to consider taking classes at your local hospital to set expectations for labor and delivery.

Chapter 2: Baby Gear

When you're expecting your first child, one of the root causes of the emotions, excitement and then overwhelming anxiety you experience at any given moment is the baby gear. For every single thing you think you might need, there are at least 25 to 50 different options. It's so easy to start thinking about what you want, wondering what you NEED and you just want to shop shop shop! You just can't wait to decorate the nursery and get your diaper bag packed! Changing station! Cute baby wall décor! Pak n Play so you can go ANYWHERE with your little bundle of joy!

So, you get a few lists from Google, you ask a girlfriend or sister, and then you go to Babies"R"Us. You sit down with your little consultant, give her your information, write your cute little message to the people (baby shower peeps) helping you equip your life and then you get your scan gun. Then you feel your stomach drop to your knees and flip flop while your significant other says "holy crap – this store is HUGE." You have 10 pages of suggestions from Babies"R"Us, two emails from relatives and a printout from the internet. You also have ten brands of bottles hanging on the wall, ten more on the shelves, and sometimes two or three options within those brands of bottles. There are different size nipples? Are you supposed to pick a nipple that most closely resembles yours? (Answer: No, the different size is the size of the hole the liquid goes through, getting bigger as baby gets bigger – so you generally start with newborn or 1 and that's the size that will come with the bottle. Look up the manufacturer to determine transition time to larger nipple sizes).

Has your husband left the store yet? Always remember – you don't have to do it all at once! Between anxiety and aching feet and backs, multiple trips and some online work is perfectly acceptable and quite common!

Fear not – while you will likely continue to consult a couple girlfriends or sisters, and still get your gigantic list from Babies"R"Us for "suggested registry items," we are going to tell you what you actually DO need. We're going to have two categories: MUST haves and NICE to haves. With ANY gift you receive, if you do not receive a gift receipt, kindly inquire as to where the gift came from in a nice way, such as "Oh this is adorable! Where did you get it? I might get a second in case a tornado sucks this one out of my hands!" We say this because you will undoubtedly register for two of one item and receive 7 – you don't need 7, so you'll be returning the other 5 for store credit or an item you can really use, and you can usually return to the big box stores as long as it still has a tag, even if you don't have the receipt.

As an aside – if you are planning on using formula, register yourself with both Enfamil and Similac (or whatever brand you PLAN on using – I say PLAN because you don't know how the baby will react and each baby reacts differently to each formula). We are telling you to register because the companies will start sending you sample cans of their formula, supplements if you're breast feeding, on-the-go packets of formula and sample bottles that are perfect for keeping a stash of necessities in (a) the car (b) your in-laws' house (c) as backup when you realize you forgot to get formula at the store yesterday and didn't realize you just used the last scoop in the house!

Nursery Furniture – the options are endless and everything will depend on the amount of room you have and how much you want in that room. Keep in mind, your walking path in the middle of the night from your room to the crib needs to be clutter- and furniture-free so plan accordingly!

| **Must Have** | Changing station – holds a few diapers, wipes, diaper rash cream, nose sucker outer, nail clippers, Vaseline and Purel. Some dressers have a changing station option that sits on top |

of the dresser, other options might be a stand-alone station. Depends on how much room you have.

Must Have Crib with slats spacing that isn't more than 2 3/8 inches (soda can) apart - no drop-sides are considered safe anymore (nor are they an option if you're buying new).

Must Have Dresser – you have to put those clothes somewhere!

Must Have Mobile or crib soother/musical toy in the crib- keeps them occupied in the mornings especially when you're getting dressed! Also – once baby is crawling and pulling herself up to her knees, she'll be able to push that button to make the crib soother start up again…Mommy can stay in bed!

Word of Caution: once your baby can stand and push that button, what makes you think they'll ONLY push it during the daytime…baby might start playing with it in the middle of the night rather than be bored and go back to sleep, even if you turn it "off" because it doesn't take a genius to learn how to turn it "on." You've been warned.

Must Have Noise machine for the room – it will play all night to "mask" any outside noises that might startle a baby awake.

Must Have Nightlight – you don't want to turn on bright light at night to change baby or feed baby nor do you want to run into the dresser, break your toe and scream "SHIT!" and startle the baby.

Must Have Rocker or chair of some sort in nursery – midnight feedings where you have to carry the baby anywhere are just hazardous! Plus, you will in fact fall asleep holding the baby – best to do so in a comfortable rocking recliner with big fat arms on either side so you don't risk

	dropping baby. So for that matter, keep a spare pillow and blanket for you beside/behind the chair.
Nice to Have	Bassinet – so you're going to need a crib (we're not touching co-sleeping but that's certainly your choice and risk) and possibly a bassinet. The crib is going to look huge when you bring your newborn home and the bassinet is portable (roll it into your room, the living room, etc…) and keeps baby nice and contained for the first couple of months.
Nice to Have	Bookshelf or cubby piece of furniture (or both).
Nice to Have	Changing station on top of dresser (one less piece of furniture in the room).
Nice to Have	Pak n Play - many have inserts for diaper changing so many people keep in their living room to have all the convenience in one spot, especially if the nursery is on a different floor than the main living area.
Nice to Have	Pak n Play mattress (if you register for this, register for fitted sheet as well).

Bedding & Blankets – You're going to be finding all kinds of bedding sets while you're decorating your nursery and those sets will come with little quilts, pillows, crib bumpers, etc… The American Academy of Pediatrics (AAP) recommends never using a bumper in the crib – again, your choice – as there's a risk of smothering if baby rolls into the bumper and can't roll away. Then again, the though of your baby smooshing her face against those slats or getting a leg caught between them (happens OFTEN), might also cause anxiety for you. You can try rolling two towels and putting them on either side of the baby (even insert a full bottle of water in the middle to give it some weight) to keep her the middle of the crib. There's some basic gear you're going to need no matter what and there are some optional items that are more convenient or structured but you could get by without them. Either way, prepare to enter the never-ending options in the world of baby gear.

Must Have	1 or 2 changing table pad covers – they are the fitted sheet thing you see on changing tables in nurseries.
Must Have	2 or 3 changing table pads (washable) - these are flat pads you lay on top of your changing table cover to protect said pad covers from poo and pee. Because, inevitably, you will get poop or pee on the pad while changing the baby.
Must Have	3 to 5 fitted crib sheets + waterproof crib mattress pad (or 2) - pillows, bumpers and blankets that come in crib bedding sets are not recommended for use until baby is able to roll back over. Why so many? Envision a 9 month old with the flu, puking everywhere. You change the bedding at midnight. At 4 a.m., there's another episode… you have to change the bedding again. See the pattern?
Must Have	Bedding for Pak n Play (Could be different size than your crib depending on what brand/style you register for).
Must Have	4 to 6 receiving blankets – anymore than that and you'll never use them, you'll just start to rotate them to try to use them. You'll do laundry every four days (really) so you'll always have a clean one. Barring a diaper explosion or Exorcist-style spit up, you'll use the same blanket for a day or two after you get over the "everything must be clean at every moment for my child!" mentality around 2 months of age.
Must Have	A loosely knit or crocheted blanket (especially for winter) that you can throw over baby, including the face, to keep the snow/rain off them when transporting if you don't get a baby-carrier cocoon. We actually

	have two that are still our go-to's even in the summer months.
Nice to Have	Bassinet bedding if you're going to use one (2 sets).
Nice to Have	Anti-rollover bumpers/positioners that keep baby in place. Economical route: two rolled towels secured with rubber bands - to keep baby from rolling over accidentally - because when they can't roll back, they get pissed and Mommy has to get up to roll baby back over.

Poop Patrol – Your life will soon be consumed by poop. Consistency and frequency of poop. The cleaning up of poop. Poop explosions. Lack of poop. UTB – Up The Back poops. UTB will inevitably occur right after bath time or right before you leave the house for a special occasion with the baby in a beautiful outfit. So here are your poop tools.

Must Have	Diapers! Check out Amazon Mom or some of the diaper subscription services you can find online. You might also save with coupons, both store and manufacturer, at local retailers and wholesale clubs. Decide if you're going to cloth or disposable. If disposable, ask around, get some opinions, and then like formula, you might have to try a few to find what works best, doesn't cause diaper rash, etc....FYI Sam's Club brand (starts at size 3 in the stores) are great and economical, as are their wipes if you don't have an ultra-sensitive skinned little one.
Must Have	Cloth or Disposable decision aside, you'll need a diaper "keeper" (most bedding sets come with one) in addition to separate hamper or service for cloth diapers. Sometimes you'll see these called diaper cubby or stacker.
Must Have	Diaper pail or something for those dirty cloth diapers.

Must Have	Diaper rash cream & Vaseline or Aquafor – the lubricants used daily can help prevent, diaper rash cream when you first notice redness. We recommend a nice supply of butt paste (looks like mud), Pink Salve or Desitin with Vaseline or Aquafor or any combination thereof. Amanda's younger sister uses Aquafor and Desitin with every change just to prevent diaper rash – it can easily develop into a yeast problem so really – keep it dry!
Must Have	If cloth diapering, 4 or 5 dozen cloth or reusable diapers.
Must Have	If cloth diapering, 8 waterproof covers.
Must Have	If cloth diapering, snaps, Velcro or safety pins to secure reusable diapers.
Must Have	If disposable diapering, one to two boxes of size 1 diapers - unless you have a preemie, the newborn size is only needed for the first week or two and you should get a pack from the hospital. A great way to stock up is to ask baby shower guests to bring a package of diapers and be entered to win a prize at the shower. Kim got so many packages of diapers at her shower, she didn't have to buy any for the first year!
Must Have	Wipes – lots of them. Really. You'll want them everywhere – in both cars, the diaper bag, baby's room, kitchen, living room. You'll want them within reach not only to clean up baby, but to clean up baby spills, baby spit-up (FYI you can use wipes to clean stains off clothes! It really works!). Some people use wipe warmers – let's get real. Unless you live in an igloo, your wipes will never be ice cold. Skip the warmers because warmth and dampness breeds germs and your breath can warm up a cold wipe in a jiffy.

Health and Safety – the extent of safety or "baby-proofing" you do in your home is going to be entirely up to you and your partner. We've got some of the basics that we found useful/life-savers – you may choose to put rubber bumpers around everything or test your child's learning curve/propensity to scar. These are just some guidelines for safety but the Health-related items are absolute!

Must Have	Humidifier – you can't use the Vick's inserts when they are very young (although Amanda used the wall plug-in versions when her 3 month old got a bad cough).
Must Have	Nipple pads (for your bra) - disposable or washable, regardless of whether you're breastfeeding, the girls will leak after birth.
Must Have	Bulb syringe - sucks out stuffy nose - use with saline spray.
Must Have	Dye- & Fragrance-Free detergent or Dreft – DO NOT CHANGE DETERGENTS!
Must Have	First Aid kit
Must Have	If breastfeeding, lanolin ointment for sore nipples
Must Have	If drying up milk, ice packs and good sports bra – we've heard cabbage leaves as well (Google it) but neither used it **if you're allergic to sulfa drugs, stay away from the cabbage leaf approach**
Must Have	multi-use thermometer
Must Have	nail clippers or scissors (might want to have 2 - one for diaper bag, one for room) – as an aside, when baby is first born, it's sometimes easier to just bite off those little nails then try to use a nail clipper on those tiny fingers. If you DO clip some finger skin (it happens) don't worry – the skin grows back! (Amanda learned this not once, not twice, but three times!)
Must Have	Nursing bras
Must Have	Teething toys
Must Have	Monitor
Nice to Have	Cupboard and drawer latches

Nice to Have	Outlet covers
Nice to Have	Toilet seat locks
Nice to Have	Safety Gates
Nice to Have	Video monitor

Clothing – ok, you're going to receive a TON of clothes! And you're going to wash all of it and put it away and get your closet and dresser all nice and organized, which you'll do about 3 to 12 times when the nesting instinct kicks in. WARNING – you will receive more clothes than you will ever use! You are going to give birth to a little human who many grow at an exponential rate or who may be stunted and wear size 6 months well into that 1st birthday. So be careful, keep tags and receipts except for those bare essentials until you know what size baby you have. Case in point – Amanda's 4 month old daughter has transitioned into size 12 months for almost everything. If someone offers you hand me downs, take them! The extras can come in handy for all occasions, leaving at grandma's house or the sitter's, etc…This list is going to get you through the first couple of months at least. Repeat for every growth spurt!

Must Have	2 to 4 Pull-on pants (with no buttons or zippers) but really, for the first 4 months or so, you'll just layer a long-sleeved and short-sleeved onesie and use a swaddling blanket to keep baby warm, not so much a sweater.
Must Have	5 to 7 long-sleeved onesies.
Must Have	5 to 7 short-sleeved onesies.
Must Have	5 t-shirts are helpful in the beginning – take them from the hospital and you're basically covered!
Must Have	8 pairs of socks.
Must Have	Keep away from the decorative clothing - big flowers, tassels, ribbons, etc… they are choking hazards and just flop into baby's face.
Must Have	Mittens – you'll find them in the baby bottle

	area at Babies"R"Us – they keep baby's hands warm as well as keep her from scratching her face with those razors called finger nails.
Must Have	One-piece "footie pajamas" or outfits (can use socks) - five to seven of these.
Must Have	Pajamas/sleepers (5 to 7): Zippers are easier to do in the middle of the night than snaps! Keep this in mind! Footed are great but if not, use socks to keep baby toasty.
Must Have	Shoes really aren't going to be necessary until the baby is really walking - you might want some decorative shoes (they also make sock shoes) but be realistic.
Must Have	You'll want a summer hat and a warm hat in the fall/winter in addition to the newborn cap.
Nice to Have	Sleeper nightgowns that are open at the bottom and pull-over mitten sleeves are great in the early weeks.

Bath time – when you first bring your munchkin home, you'll be doing sponge baths until that umbilical cord stump falls off. Even to give a sponge bath, though, an infant bathing tub with insert that you can lay the baby on is a back-saver! You'll be able to get away with bathing in that tub on the counter until around month five or six (or if you have a big baby, four months in Amanda's case) and then you'll probably have to move into the bathtub.

Must Have	3 soft hooded baby towels.
Must Have	8 to 12 washcloths - you'll use in the bath as well as to wipe baby's face in the mornings.
Must Have	Baby soap/shampoo and lotion.
Must Have	baby soft-bristled hair brush and comb - great for cradle cap (if these are provided at the hospital, snag 'em!).
Must Have	rubbing alcohol (clean the thermometer as well as dry up umbilical cord).
Nice to Have	Infant bath tub.

Meal Time – there are many different kinds and methods and timings of feeding: breastfeeding or formula, starting on baby food, making your own baby food, when to start, how to start, what to feed. KISS (Keep It Super Simple) and as always, consult your pediatrician before changing your baby's diet. Either way, prepare to dedicate a cupboard to Junior.

Must Have	4 to 6 4oz bottles, 4 to 6 8oz bottles plus for sitter/daycare - plus next size nipples.
Must Have	6 to 8 burp cloths - can also just use cloth diapers.
Must Have	Baby spoons: A rubber-tipped or plastic spoon is easier on your baby's gums and small enough to fit easily into a little mouth.
Must Have	Bottle brush.
Must Have	Bottles may come with white caps - keep them! You'll need when you're making formula for cereal.
Must Have	Bowls: Some parents like baby bowls with suction cups on the bottom – these stick to the tray and resist being flung to the floor.
Must Have	Highchair or booster chair you can strap to a dining room chair or use on a counter.
Must Have	If breastfeeding, breast pump.
Must Have	If breastfeeding, breast milk storage bags or containers.
Must Have	If breastfeeding, nursing bras and possibly tops.
Must Have	LOTS OF BIBS - I'm talking at least 10 and I probably have 20 in the rotation - between drooling, feedings, spitting up, general soaking, we probably go through 20 a week!
Must Have	Sippy cups (3 to 5): These cups come with a lid and a spout for easy drinking. And (the real plus) they don't spill when knocked over. Cups with handles will probably be easiest for your child to manage at first. Avoid cups with attached straws

	– they're hard to clean and spill easily. If you're concerned about BPA, phthalates, and other chemicals in plastics, alternatives abound, including reusable metal water bottles small enough for a baby's hands.
Must Have	Starter sippy cup - usually has handles on both sides and a mouth spout that is similar to a bottle.
Must Have	Bottle drying rack.
Nice to Have	Package or 3 of pre-made 2oz and 6oz bottles in the formula of your choice for that first week or so – until you get the hang of things, the pre-made bottles are life savers – just shake and serve and save yourself until week 2 for bottle washing. **make sure you get nipples for those bottles!**
Nice to Have	Boppie pillow for feeding – you can use your couch pillows but boppie is great as they get bigger to prop them up, help with sitting and tummy time.
Nice to Have	Bottle sterilizer (Or when you get tired of hand washing 8 bottles a day, you can keep a Tupperware container with sudsy water throughout the day, replenish, rinse. Dishwasher works just fine).

Sleeping/Soothing – you remember all that sleep you weren't getting in your last month of pregnancy? Well, there are tools to help baby sleep so you can sleep too – otherwise you're going to start looking like an old fashioned burglar with a built-in dark under-eye circles mask. These tools will help keep baby soothed for a longer period of time. Plus – there are times that babies just cry. And cry, and cry and cry. Swings and bouncers can be life savers!

Must Have	Pacifiers (also called binkies) – careful on these, they don't always take to them, so see if baby takes the hospital pacifier before you

unpack all the new ones you'll get. Also, after taking one brand for so long (wasn't tapered, it's very similar to hospital pacifier, Sam won't take the cute baseball, football binkies people got us). Use those straps that clip to baby's clothes or carrier straps but NEVER keep them connected when baby is sleeping!

Must Have	Bouncy seat or bouncer.
Must Have	Sound machine.
Must Have	Swaddling blankets - when you swaddle, the baby will not be in a sleeper or footie pajamas or even a onesie because you risk over-heating. If it's winter time, you might want to use a t-shirt in the early weeks to keep that little bit of exposed skin on the chest warm.
Must Have	Swing – one that goes both directions – side to side and front to back, all kinds of settings & plugs in!
Nice to Have	Wearable blankets or sleep sacks
Nice to Have	Swaddling contraption ie: SwaddleMe or the Miracle Blanket (we both used & loved)

Transportation – you're going to need some essentials to even take baby home from the hospital and eventually you will even dare to take the baby with you out in public. These will help you do that.

Must Have	Car base for each car. Your local BMV should have free Identity stickers for the carrier/bases. (In case of an accident).
Must Have	Heavy duty stroller - sometimes it comes with your infant carrier.
Must Have	Infant carrier for car.
Must Have	Umbrella stroller.

Nice to Have	Baby Bjorn / body carrier of some sort.
Nice to Have	Sling – only if you can figure out how to use it – we never could!
Nice to Have	Sun shade for backset car windows.

Diaper Bag – When you do finally venture outside your home with Junior, you're going to need a diaper bag. You want something that both you and your partner are comfortable carrying and has lots of pockets and compartments and room. Your days of dainty handbags are over; you are now a pack mule.

Must Have	At least 4 diapers.
Must Have	Changing pad (usually comes with the bag, you might want a couple disposable ones too just in case).
Must Have	Diaper rash ointment, baby Tylenol, gas drops.
Must Have	Extra outfit or two – especially during times of teething, explosive poops can be constant!
Must Have	If formula feeding, you'll want a couple bottles with enough formula for 2 to 3 feedings.
Must Have	Package of wipes.
Must Have	Poopy diaper bags - like doggie poop bags.
Must Have	Spare pacifier and small toy/rattle.
Must Have	Ziploc bag for soiled clothes (keep a clean change of clothes in it).

Play time! You're going to want (and will receive) some basic activity items for your munchkin because even at an early age (weeks old) you'll want to start tummy time and engage the baby's senses when he is actually awake.

Must Have	Play Mat/Gym - Activity mat for the floor.
Must Have	Soft toys, rattles, musical toys.

Nice to Have	Play yard - we affectionately call ours the cage but honestly, it's a great way to pen off a section of your living or family room, put some toys and baby inside and walk away. It lets you get dinner ready without chasing the crawler and keeps baby safe from climbing onto the dog. Or fireplace.
Nice to Have	Soft or board books - Highlights "Hello" is a great education/reading program – safe for baby **and** durable! *Friends/Family can **GIFT** you subscriptions that you can adjust as baby grows.
Nice to Have	Bath Toys and eventually a bath "mat" to keep baby in place in the tub once he can sit up.
Nice to Have	Jumparoo or Exer-saucer – might also be called stationary jumper or stationary activity station.
Nice to Have	Bumbo or some other seat with a tray – helps them start sitting up and keeps them from falling over. They won't do well in the highchair until at least 6 months old, but you can start them in the bumbo around 4 months.

So those are your basics – are you overwhelmed yet? Try registering for all this stuff – you'll get a cramp in your trigger hand! Just take it easy and remember you can register at multiple stores and make multiple trips to those stores plus you can usually add/subtract from your registry online.

Some shortcuts we recommend (and as always, when in doubt, consult your pediatrician!):

Sensitive formula – Register with Enfamil and Gerber and any other brand of formula to get their freebies, including Enfamil Gentlease formula. The samples are great for grandma's house, emergency backup, etc… Sam's Club has their own version of Enfamil Gentlease and we've both used it, no issues, especially with the $17/tub savings!

Car carrier – buy strap cushions at least if not also a head pillow for the carrier. Those straps cut right into baby's cheeks and neck – the cushions just strap on with Velcro usually and keep their faces cushioned.

Snowsuits – unless you are going for a walk in Anchorage, Alaska or plan to build a snowman with your infant, you really aren't going to use these. The baby won't fit in the carrier in one and will overheat in about 2 minutes. They are completely unnecessary and ridiculous.

Generic is A-OK when it comes to baby food. Often times, it's made by the same manufacturer as the name-brand food!

As your baby gets older and is actually interactive – around 6 months old – you'll need to start considering the baby safety precautions for your home and more interactive toys. To stockpile them before then, unless someone gives them to you, just adds more clutter to your home.

Chapter 3: Selecting a Pediatrician

When it comes to selecting a pediatrician, you want to find one that works well within your parenting style. For instance, if you are not breastfeeding, you will want to find a pediatrician who won't give you a guilt trip about formula every time you go in with your baby. Also, if you want some flexibility with immunizations or will want to skip some altogether, you'll want to find a pediatrician who is flexible and respects your decision about immunizations as well. Interviews are entirely appropriate and most pediatricians have open times in the afternoons one or two days a week specifically for meeting with new parents. You have to find someone with whome you are 150% comfortable with because they will be caring for your baby, you'll be relying upon them for advice on the health of your baby AND you will be seeing the doctor A LOT in the first year!

You should pick a doctor or practice who is conveniently located between the home, the sitter and your office as you coordinate appointments with your work schedule. Ask your local friends who are moms to see who they have had good experiences with and would who they would recommend. Maybe you want someone who is mid-career and has some children themselves or you would prefer a woman over a man. You'll definitely want to make sure the pediatrician is covered by your insurance network. You'll want to know if you'll always see your selected pediatrician or if there are partners in the office you might have to see in emergencies. Does their office keep a certain number of slots open each day for sick kids?

You should start this process during the early stages of your pregnancy because you may find some are not taking new patients, which may prolong your search. When you get to the hospital for delivery, they are going to ask you for the name of your pediatrician. Some pediatricians will come to the hospital within a day or two of delivery to examine the baby, and some will defer to the pediatrician on staff at the hospital for this first visit, and then you'll take the baby to the pediatrician a week after birth.

Typically, you'll have appointments with your pediatrician at 1 week, 2 months, 4 months, 6 months, 9 months and 12 months in the first year, plus any illnesses that might pop up. The good news is, the wellness checks at the time periods we listed above are usually free and covered fully by insurance and the doctor doesn't even require a co-pay or office visit charge. So you really have no reason to NOT take your baby for well-checks! When you're preparing for a doctor's visit, it's perfectly OK to write down the questions you have as you'll never remember them. If you're taking more than one child for a doctor's visit, you really might want some help. It's hard enough taking one baby in the infant carrier plus your purse plus your diaper bag, let alone another kid!

There is a lot a controversy out there around the vaccinations for infants and circumcisions for boys – we are both mainstream, so we follow the recommended immunization schedule. If you have differing views, you need to determine your plan and then find a doctor who is willing to work with you.

Chapter 4: Labor, Delivery & Hospital

So you've made it. You made it through swollen "cankles," throwing up in the kitchen sink, peeing in every gas station between home and work, survived tons of needles and blood work and muddle through hospital pre-registration and education classes. You've grown breasts the size of a cabbage patch kid doll's head, sneeze peed at least once, repacked the diaper bag at least twice and reorganized the baby's room three times thanks to that insane nesting instinct. So now what?

Well, let's have a baby! It's a scientific fact that the last four weeks of pregnancy evolved just to get mothers to the point that they didn't care if it took forceps from Hellraiser to get that baby out, she just wanted to give birth and as such, didn't fear it as much as she did in the first trimester (ok, it's not scientific fact, it's just how you'll feel). I promise – by the 42nd one way or another, that child will make its presence known week (yes, some doctors make you go 2 weeks past your due date before they'll induce your labor and get that sucker out). Oh – and the fallacy, yes fallacy, that first time pregnancies tend to deliver early, on time, late – all bullshit. The baby will come when the baby will come. So just get ready and then wait…

As you start your 8th month, you're going to start paying attention to the signs of impending labor. You'll start to wonder if everything you're experiencing is a sign of labor. Because trust us, once you reach "fully baked" at 38 to 39 weeks, you'll want to get that child out. Some signs that your body is getting ready for its own personal Alien-style scene:

Braxton Hicks contractions – you may have been experiencing these already. They sort of feel like quick, strong cramps that come and go at totally irregular intervals. It's hard to really explain what they feel like, other than they feel like nothing else you have experienced yet and you just KNOW it's not a ligament pain or cramp. It's MORE. The thing to remember is that if there's no regular pattern both in length and frequency, you're experiencing Braxton Hicks. Anything with a regular pattern of getting longer in duration, stronger and closer together (more frequent) over the course of an hour and it's time to start thinking about the hospital and getting things in order.

Your cervix starts to change as labor is approaching. Basically, it starts to soften in preparation of letting that baby pass through. You may also lose your mucus plug or notice what is called "bloody show" which is cervical mucus with some pink or red tinge to it. Your mucus plug has developed over the course of your pregnancy to seal off your cervical canal to keep infection out of the uterus and keep baby safe. If you lose it, you know by the gelatinous blob with perhaps a tinge of brown ick.

If your water breaks, and it might trickle a bit or be more like "wow I'm really peeing myself," it's time for the hospital because then you're running against the clock because that amniotic fluid is what's been protecting the baby against infection this whole time – so don't monkey around if that happens!

By your 8th month, you should have a set of guidelines from your doctor or caregiver, as well as from the hospital where you'll deliver the baby, as to when to call the doctor or go to the hospital. General guidelines could include:

- If it's been an uncomplicated pregnancy, contractions lasting about a minute each and coming every five minutes for at least an hour. If you're high-risk, though, your caregiver may want to hear from as soon as you think you are having contractions.

- If you're unsure of what's going on or just don't feel right, the 8th month of pregnancy is NOT the time to "wait and see." Just give your doctor a call and get guidance. It's what you're paying them for. If you aren't feeling the baby move regularly – call your doctor. Decreased fetal movement during pregnancy (you should feel at least 10 movements every hour) can be a cause for concern.
- When you start feeling what you think are "real" contractions, start tracking them and writing down everything – when you do call your doctor or hospital, they're going to ask you some typical questions such as how close together the contractions are, how long they last, how strong (ie: can you talk "through" a contraction) and any other symptoms you may be experiencing so write it all down because in the middle of the excitement and fear of the baby actually coming, you will have massive brain farts and barely remember your address, let alone details about the contractions.
- DEFINITELY call your doctor and/or head to the hospital in the following situations:
  - If your water breaks or you think you're leaking amniotic fluid – if you see traces of yellow, brown or green, that could signal the presence of meconium, your baby's first stool and that can be bad – get to the hospital pronto!
  - If your baby has been less active – in the last month of pregnancy, your baby is running out of room so the hyper-activity you've been feeling may diminish a bit. However, you should still feel at least 10 movements every hour. If you haven't, try having

some juice or eating something to give the baby a "jump." If that doesn't help, go to the hospital right away.

- o If you have vaginal bleeding beyond "bloody show" (mucus with a spot or streak of blood), constant and severe abdominal pain or a fever.
- o If you are having contractions before the 37th week of pregnancy or other signs of preterm labor.
- o Symptoms of preeclampsia such as severe headaches, blurry vision, abnormal swelling sudden increase in intensity. If you have any of these symptoms anyways, you are likely under the close supervision of your doctor so do as you're told.

If it's been determined it's time for the hospital, grab a towel (protect the car seat), your hospital bag (more on that later), your driver (please don't drive yourself) and go to the hospital. You'll get checked in and it will take about an hour to get settled into your room, hooked up to all the machines and seen by three interns and four nurses (unless you have a child emerging from your vagina and if that's the case, skip to Delivery now) but not your doctor. Your doctor is going to be kept informed as to your progress from the hospital staff, but unless there's a body coming out of you, the doctor won't arrive until you're around 8 cm dilated and really close to actual delivery.

If your doctor has determined that your little bundle just isn't going to start this process on his own and you need to be induced, you will go through the same hour of setup work as you would for a normal delivery. Then you will be hooked up to an IV of an induction drug, maybe some pitocin too, and then you will wait 12 hours. Once the drug is started, by the way, you don't get to go pee in the bathroom; you get to use a bedpan. Yes it sucks but you get over it because remember, you're still VERY pregnant and you still have to pee A LOT and they are pumping you full of fluids. Twelve hours after you're induced, they'll check your cervix to see if anything fun has happened. Hopefully it has.

Generally speaking, if you are dilated 3 centimeters and having regular contractions, you now qualify for the epidural! You may decide to go the all natural route – go for it. We say, to each her own. The spinal tap, we will admit, is not a walk in the park, but neither are contractions. AND once you get the epidural, you have to be catheterized because, well, you're numb from the waist down and you don't know if you have to pee or not. So keep in mind, if you want to try some walking or ball exercises or any other way to get through the pain that involves your legs, you can't get an epidural because you won't be able to feel your legs!

And you know that birth plan we talked about in Chapter 1? The one we said you might have to deviate from for a safe delivery? You may want to do a natural or vaginal childbirth but circumstances may dictate otherwise – such as if the baby or you are suddenly in distress, you might have to undergo an emergency c-section. Or, you may be thinking you want an epidural the whole time but baby is coming too fast to administer it. Please try to always remember you have only one goal – safe delivery of a healthy baby. The means to that end are irrelevant in the grand scheme of things!

You will basically be doted on by your partner and the nurses the whole time you are in labor. You will also not be allowed to eat anything beyond popsicles (another reason to not head to the hospital TOO soon because you don't get to eat!) and crushed ice but honestly, you're in labor and food isn't exactly the first thing on your mind. You may also permit the interns or other medical personnel to do exams on you to check your dilation and other such fun. Yes, it will feel and appear that they are indeed sticking their entire arms, up to their elbows, into your vaginal canal. Your partner will be amazed and you will be irritated and uncomfortable. Sometimes you get the trifecta, especially if you're getting close and your doctor is there, because you'll get the nurse, the intern and then they'll call the doctor so he/she can get an arm in too. By then you're pretty certain that if someone would just try a little they could just grab that little bugger's head and pull him out already.

Technically speaking, there are three stages of labor & delivery so we'll review those quickly. If you're a first-timer, your hospital should provide some birthing class preparation course that will walk you, and your birthing partner, through the whole routine and show you the birthing ward. ASK QUESTIONS – ask anything. Chances are, someone else in that class was also wondering if you might poop on the table. Or if it's true that you bleed even if you have a c-section.

EARLY LABOR: The longest phase of labor is the first stage – it's where your body gets ready to go into full labor. Your cervix will start to dilate up to 3 centimeters and you start having mild to moderate contractions that last anywhere from 30 to 45 seconds and occur at five to 20 minute intervals. If you lose your mucus plug you may have what is called bloody show (bloody discharge) as well. The contractions may feel more like cramps or a backache until the last few hours of early labor when you're REALLY noticing the regularity and severity of the contractions. Don't go rushing off to the hospital just yet – just start paying attention, tracking the frequency and length of the contractions and make sure you have everything you need for your pending hospital stay. You don't want to rush immediately if you don't have to because the comforts of home (no machines, no IV's, etc...) are always more relaxing than the clinical atmosphere of the hospital. Eat a light snack because once you're in the hospital in labor, food is not an option. Go for a little walk to keep labor progressing and give yourself something to do before you're stuck in a bed for the next day or so. Go to the hospital when your contractions are more frequent (5 to 10 minutes apart) or painful – or, go when you WANT to go because it's ALWAYS your choice to go to the hospital whenever you feel you need to!

ACTIVE LABOR: Phase 2 is the hospital phase – meaning, you better be at the hospital by now! Your cervix continues to dilate to 7 cm as your contractions increase in their intensity, length (40 to 60 seconds) and frequency (every three to four minutes). This phase is usually just a couple to four hours long. Walking is probably not going to be an option much longer, so trade that in for a cool washcloth on your forehead or neck, backrubs and breathing exercises. Nurses will be monitoring your vitals as well as the baby's so you'll be getting poked and prodded (up their elbows or so it seems) a lot. Stay focused on the fact that you're about to hold your baby! If you want an epidural and haven't already had one, this is your window of opportunity. Once you're in Advanced Labor, it's too late and you're just going to have to Superwoman through it. Remember that Birthing Plan? Toss it out the window and do whatever you need to do!

ADVANCED LABOR: This is your push time – typically it's 15 minutes to an hour of actual, hard-core, push and get that baby out! Your cervix has dilated to 10 cm, your room is a flurry of activity and your contractions are INTENSE and FREQUENT (almost feeling nonstop but they're probably a couple minutes apart – it's just that the peaks are so intense that you feel like you haven't rested yet when the next one is starting).   You will start to feel that intense pressure in your backside – lower back and rectum, you may get nauseous (hence, you're not allowed food once you're at the hospital), get the shakes, get the chills or get really sweaty. By now, you're probably over it. You're tired, you're overwhelmed, you're anxious – you're almost there though! Don't push until someone tells you too because pushing too soon can cause complications during delivery.

Once you see the nurses uncover the bassinet and all the medical goodies, start up the warmer and move some things around, you know you're close to go time! Now you're getting excited and your partner is starting to sweat because holy shit balls fatherhood is upon us! Ignore him and concentrate on yourself.

Amanda had two C-sections while Kim delivered all three of her girls vaginally. Nothing can really prepare you for what you're going to go through because, like everything else that involves a baby, it's different for every single mother for every single baby. You don't get to push until you're fully dilated and that baby is finally ready to exit. Some of the signs that you're ready besides the frantic activity in the room may include a burning sensation or this urge to poop – yup, that's right, we said poop. You bear down as though you are having the biggest bowel movement of your life (this will ACTUALLY happen a couple days later but we digress). What you're feeling is that basketball (ok, it just FEELS like it's a basketball but it's more like a softball) right at your vagina, waiting to come out and see you. When you hear someone tell you to start pushing, you want to feel as though you're pooping – and yes, it's true, you might poop. But there's going to be a whole lot of mess coming out of your body and the nurses and doctor do not care – it all gets swept aside with everything else. You have one focus – push the basketball OUT!

If you've had an epidural, you may feel some slight pressure but not a lot of anything else – so you're relying more on what the nurses tell you to do rather than what your BODY may be trying to tell you to do. As the baby starts to pass through, remember, you're pushing what FEELS like a basketball out of what you thought was a small vagina… so all that stretching and pulling is going to burn and not feel good. But if your baby is right there, waiting to get pushed out, you don't have far to go so just push! And Breathe. And Push. And Breathe. Somehow, we were built for this.

Now – remember, until the baby is out of you, anything can happen. You might go through 27 hours of labor (12 hours of induction, 15 hours of active labor) and reach 9 centimeters of dilation only to find that suddenly, your daughter has decided that she doesn't REALLY want to come out to play and she starts regressing. Yup – you can actually LOSE your dilation! Or come up with any possible scenario that leads to an emergency c-section. Welcome to my world.

So if the doctor does decide that a c-section is the way to go, stay calm. It just means you aren't pushing the basketball out of you, it's going to come out through a life-long scar because fate decided you should NEVER forget that you ever had a baby. So what will happen is that you will get your machines mobilized and your partner will be escorted with you down to the operating room. Your partner will be taken to a different room and dressed into his own scrubs while you get prepped, which will include being placed onto an operating table, hooked up to some more machines and covered in toasty warm blankets because between the shock to your body and the morphine shakes and the temperature of the OR being about 43 degrees, you're shaking nonstop and freezing your numb ass off.

If you haven't had an epidural already, they may opt for a spinal block. It honestly just depends on your doctor and timing. Either measure is to ensure that you are not feeling anything besides a bit of pressure as they get the baby out, and if you take education classes at the hospital, you'll watch both a vaginal and surgical birth so I'll spare you the details. Both your view and that of your partner's will be hidden by a blue screen so you won't witness anything. Once the baby is out, they'll suck the mucus out of the airway and then congratulations! Baby's here! You'll get to see the baby before they take it over to the other side of the room to clean her up and get her warm and take all their measurements and run a couple tests run on all babies in the first minutes they're born.

You're going to be a bit out of it, given the morphine drip that you're now on, but your partner will bring the baby over to you so you can see her and kiss her for the first time. Go ahead and cry, I think everyone does. Once they get you closed up (they have to stitch both your uterus and your abdomen) they'll roll you into recovery and bring you your baby. At that moment – time stops. You are suddenly gazing at the most beautiful baby you have ever seen and you can hardly breathe. Congratulations – you're a mommy!

Once you're up and around, feel free to take a shower, wash your hair, put on your makeup and start to feel human again. If you've been catheterized, they'll usually remove the catheter the next morning, and have you measure your first couple of tinkles to ensure everything's working properly. As soon as you can go to the bathroom unsupervised, start asking for stool softeners if they haven't been offered. Think about the last time you had a bowel movement…some hospitals may not release you until you have your first one, others will send you home with orders to follow up with your doctor if it doesn't happen within a day or two of coming home. Either way – you need those stool softeners. Drugs, IV's and the trauma you've just put your body through will, well, stop you up and when it's finally time to go, it can be like giving birth again IF you don't take some precautions, like those stool softeners.

Most hospitals may give you a girdle or abdominal wrap to wear and take home – in conjunction with nurses coming in to press on your abdomen to see if your upper intestine can make its way out of your vagina (joke), the girdle is also helping to keep the pressure on and force all the remnants of pregnancy out of you and get your uterus to go back to its normal size. You're going to be bleeding hardcore for awhile – as in weeks. And for the first week or two, that girdle may be your new friend.

Recovery from a c-section may be a bit longer than vaginal, given the morphine and all, but once you're able to walk to the bathroom and pee, they'll remove your catheter and then basically, you're on your own! Your partner can bring you whatever you want to eat and drink (coffee is bliss) and you can shower, wash your hair, put on makeup, accept visitors but most importantly, you can snuggle and hold your baby all damn day long if you want to!

You really can't hold your baby too much in the first couple weeks – so don't think you're going to spoil her at all. So go ahead and hold her. You're going to have visitors who want to hold the baby and that policy is up to you – definitely just ask that everyone wash or Purel their hands first. Whether or not you keep the baby in the room with you 24/7 or if you send him to the nursery at night is totally your call. If you're breastfeeding, they will bring the baby to you to nurse throughout the night. If you're bottle feeding, the nurses will love giving the baby a bottle. The baby will always be transported in a moving bassinet so you can keep him by your side through the night quite safely. Amanda recommends sending the little one to the nursery. You are about to not sleep through the night for weeks or months – get some shuteye while you can. If you wake up early, you can always, at any hour, go to the nursery and ask them to give you your baby.

If you deliver vaginally, you may only spend one or two nights in the hospital. If you have a c-section, you usually spend 2 nights. If you get induced and have a c-section, you might be there for three nights because they'll usually induce you overnight and then you stay 3 nights following the c-section. For example, Amanda was induced Wednesday night. Her daughter Samantha was born 9:30 Thursday night. She wasn't discharged until Sunday afternoon. Which leads us into the last big mystery of labor and delivery, and that's the hospital stay!

Chapter 5: Staying at the hospital

The length of your stay and subsequently the amount of "make yourself at home" crap you want to bring to the hospital will depend on how long you're there. Do you need every comfort of home or can you keep it minimal? Do you think you'll want to wash your hair (yes) and put on some make-up? Do you think you'll wear the hospital gown the whole time (no) or want some comfy lounge clothes (yes)? So let's talk about the essentials that you'll want to bring with you (and this will depend on the facility too because each one is different. This list is based on you getting a private room with in-suite bathroom and shower).

Think of your hospital stay as a weekend getaway in a secluded cabin – you don't want to bring the kitchen sink, but you want to have some things on hand to keep you comfortable (remember, if you're in the hospital, chance are there's a drugstore and food nearby so anyone could bring you something if you forget it or decide you need it). So essentials for the hospital will include:

- Your photo ID and insurance card
- Your birth plan if you have one
- Key phone numbers written down – both sets of grandparents-to-be, best friends, siblings. Now is not the time to assume your husband has all those numbers in his phone. Just write them down.
- Your focus object if you're going to try to go natural/vaginal
- Watch or small clock with second hand to time contractions
- Soft fabric headband or rubber bands for your hair – you know how the plastic or bigger headbands start to hurt your

head after about 4 hours? Picture yourself in your 10th hour of labor grabbing that sucker off your head, snapping it in half and throwing it at your husband. Stick with something that will keep your bangs and hair off your face and not make you psycho.

- Eyeglasses/spare contacts – at some point, you may want to just take out your contacts or need to for medical purposes. Have enough pairs for a 3 day stay or a back up pair in case something happens. You know how you felt on that one trip when you realized you tore a contact and had 7 days before you'd be home?
- Slippers/socks. Yes, the hospital gives you some basic pairs of socks with the grips – just pick up a pair of easy slippers or bring from home. No flip flops (hospital floors are slippery) please. Also – after you have the baby, your feet will be swelling to what looks like twice their size – so to go home, plan accordingly. Those slippers might be what you wear home because even your slip-on shoes won't fit!
- If you're going natural and think you'll be walking the halls during early labor, you might want to bring a robe to ward off the chill and keep your backend covered.
- iPod/iPad/mp3 player for some tunes/distraction and their charge cords. Most hospitals have wireless internet (wifi) you'll be able to tap into plus televisions in the room.
- Magazines or Books for both you and your partner
- Cell phone and charger
- Toiletries – at some point, you will be able to try to feel human again – feel free to bring a travel shampoo/conditioner, razor, hair brush, make-up, etc… Leave the perfume at home – your new baby is going to be

very sensitive to lotions and perfumes that he comes in contact with so lotions should not be scented either.

- Your partner will want some comfy shoes and maybe a change of clothing and deodorant. Unless he doesn't sweat under the pressure of his beloved wife trying to break his fingers as she endures her 109th contraction and he's just seen her water break all over the bed and where the hell is that intern's arm going?!
- CAMERA! Video camera if you choose as well, chargers or backup batteries and make sure there's room on that memory card!
- Snacks – for your partner, sorry. Remember, you're not eating during labor.
- Money – change and small bills for vending machines.
- Fresh nightgown or PJ's after delivery because the last thing you want is your itchy hospital gown. Yoga pants, a tank top and a nice soft long cardigan are pretty standard attire in the maternity ward. Don't forget slippers (that you may just want to leave in the trash....start thinking about what's been on the floor in the hospital and you won't want to bring them home).
- If you're going to be nursing, you'll want a nursing bra right off, unless you want to be topless for every Tom, Dick & Harry and doctor who will be coming in to see you.
- Bring your big granny panties, honey. After you have the baby, you still look about 6 months pregnant at least. Keep that in mind for your comfy clothes for the hospital stay and your going-home outfit too. Those slim jeans aren't going to fit just yet. And you're going to be bleeding – a lot. The hospital will give you their sexy mesh underwear to keep

those gigantic pads in place but there's something about just wearing your own. Amanda even wore both at the same time!

- Your nurses are going to ask you about the baby's stools, frequency of bowel movements and pee diapers and how much or how long baby is eating. So a small notepad and pen will be handy to bring with you. Amanda used an app on her iPhone and continued to use it until about the time she went back to work, as she was also putting her daughter on a schedule. Get used to tracking pee diapers, poop diapers and feedings – frequency and quantity, as your pediatrician will ask about those at every visit.

- A going home outfit for Mama and Baby. Remember – you still look pregnant. And your feet look like the Incredible Hulk's. Baby's outfit should coincide with the season and you'll soon learn you always want some sort of blanket, light or heavy, covering baby. The rule of thumb is one more layer than you need for yourself.

- Make sure that car seat base is installed – on the day you're discharged, you won't be allowed to leave the hospital with the baby unless the nurse who is wheeling you out see's baby in a car seat and a base in your car.

Leave your jewelry, cashed paycheck and over the counter medications (the hospital can provide anything you might need from that perspective) at home. You don't need to bring diapers as the hospital will provide diapers, swaddling blankets, t-shirts and burp cloths for baby during your stay. You don't need to bring a breast pump either – if for some reason you need to pump, the hospital will provide one for you to use.

At home, make sure you have a healthy supply of big sanitary pads – because you're going to bleed for a few weeks after delivery. It varies from person to person, but plan on about 3 weeks of it. AND – it doesn't matter if you have a c-section or vaginal birth, you still bleed the same. And you can't use tampons during this time period – honestly, you don't even want to because you're bleeding so heavily. Plus you're continuing to wear the girdle/abdomen compression contraption you wore at the hospital to try to flatten your uterus back to normal so plan on those yoga pants and t-shirts as your standard wardrobe for the first week or two.

TAKE HOME FROM HOSPITAL

Bulb Syringe

All t-shirts

2oz bottles of formula and nipples (if not breastfeeding)
Receiving blankets – best for swaddling newborns because standard swaddling blankets are HUGE!
Hospital pacifier

Really – you're getting charged for it once it's in your rolling bassinet/cabinet-o-supplies in your birthing room, and even when you leave, the nurse will have you clean it out, so take it. You will use it all!

Chapter 6: First Month aka Mommy Zombie

Believe it or not, the hospital is actually going to send you home with this brand new human being just a couple days after you give birth. They must be crazy! Nope, they aren't crazy, you're crazy to leave the hospital! No, really, it will be ok. Let's talk about your first month home with the baby.

We already touched on the three week period you're going to have, regardless of how you've delivered. And yes, it's true, you need to use pads. Give your vagina a break. You're also going to notice that, suddenly, you're peeing A LOT when you go to the bathroom. There's nothing wrong, your bladder is just no longer the size of a pee, being squished by an 8 pound baby, so you actually have normal urinary function again – yay!

Around your 2nd or 3rd day home, you're going to have the big one. Remember how we said that you need to ask for stool softeners when you're in the hospital? The nurses will even tell you to make sure you have some at home. TAKE THEM! As soon as you get that baby out and you're able to walk to the bathroom, start popping stool softeners. Amanda's big one post-Samantha hit Christmas morning (her daughter was born December 20th). All dressed and ready to leave to visit with the brand new baby when it hits – the colon has spoken, it's time for that first bowel movement.

Now, you may not want to read this or think about it, but you need to. This is going to be the worst poop of your life. Your partner needs to take charge of the baby and you need to be comfortable because it may take awhile. You haven't pooped since you had the baby – think of how many days that has been. You've had pain killers, possibly birthing drugs and then a bombardment of whatever food you haven't been able to eat during your pregnancy and labor – caffeine, sugar, proteins…. And nothing has exited your body yet. You're about to give birth to a giant hard piece of poo. You're going to get nervous as you start to realize you haven't had a bowel movement for a week – it's ok, it really will come out. You don't want to bear down too hard or you're going to pop three more hemorrhoids. But it is going to hurt from the perspective of a large hard log of poop coming out of your rectum – hence the stool softeners. A warm washcloth might help ease the way, and a glass of cold water might keep you cool because you may very well work up a sweat – you think we're kidding, but we're not. You can also try rocking back and forth on the porcelain throne a bit to help, well, get it out. The good news is, once you pass that sucker, you suddenly feel five pounds lighter and will be full of energy, considering the fact you just gave rectal birth to your baby's five pound poop twin.

After you've survived your first poop, you're going to experience some serious sleep deprivation – it definitely happens to everyone, you will be NO exception. You just have to remember, it is temporary and you will get back to a normal sleep schedule soon. See our section on Sleeping Baby – then re-read our section on Sleeping Baby. Because a sleeping baby means a sleeping mama! Honestly, you might feel like you sleep more with the baby out of you (no more hourly pee breaks throughout the night, you can suddenly sleep on your stomach – it's heaven!) but after about 5 days, you're going to realize that you don't know what day it is. And there's a container of food in the fridge but you don't know where it came from. It's ok – you're just in what we like to call Zombie Mama mode. You're doing everything to keep the baby healthy and fed and clean and you're just surviving. Good Job! That's all you need to do for the first month. If you're lucky, some friends and family are dropping off dinners so you don't have to cook and you're getting more gifts for the baby – always fun!

After you bring home the baby, everyone you know is going to want to come over for a visit. And for the first few days, you're going to think you're actually up for this. Soon though, you're going to realize you're not and that's ok. You might start to get upset that other people are holding your baby for an hour and you're not – and that's ok too. Because YOU'RE the one who carried that sucker for 40 weeks and if you want to hold him constantly, you go girl – you earned it! People are always so very excited for a brand new baby but it's perfectly ok for you to say (after they wash their hands to take the baby), "here you go for a few minutes, but then I really want him back." He belongs to you and your partner and no one else. You will, in fact, feel an insane, jealous, primordial motherly instinct of "get your hands off my baby" every time anyone is holding your child. Blame the hormones. And hold your baby.

The hormones haven't quite gone away just yet just because you've had the baby. In fact, sorry, but it may take months before you feel completely back to normal. You might continue to sob during the newest Muppets movie, or want to kill your mother-in-law, sucker-punch your husband, look at your baby and just cry with uncontrollable joy or want to kill the grocery clerk who asks when you're due….with the baby right there in the cart. It's A-OK. It's called hormones. It took 40 weeks to get those suckers all geared up – they aren't going to settle down overnight! Same goes for your body – the first month home is not the time to start a major diet or workout routine. You have very simple goals – feed baby, sleep baby, change baby. There are no other expectations.

So when you have visitors coming over – first, ask them to come at a time that's good for YOU and baby. And don't worry about what you look like – they don't care. They want the baby. So use that time to take a shower. Or a nap. If they're really good friends or family, they'll come over bearing food and will ask where your sweeper is and they'll pick up around the house for you. Because when people offer you help – TAKE IT. You shouldn't be trying to do it all anyways and remember, you're in Zombie Mama mode.

You don't even know your address at this point. Let people help you so you can catch up on sleep.

Speaking of which – if the baby is sleeping, you should be sleeping. Yes – everyone has told you – "when the baby sleeps, you sleep." But you continue to say "but, I want to [fill in the blank]. No! Sleep! This is your rule every day in the first month or else you're going to try to put the baby back up in your vagina because you will feel that is the only way to get some sleep.   I don't care if it's 9:00 a.m. and the baby just went down – take a nap. 2:00 p.m. and the baby was only up for 2 hours? Take a nap. 6:00 p.m. and the baby is napping? So are you. You are going to be up all night with this child, feeding her every two or three hours – where in that knowledge can you not find the wisdom in sleeping throughout the day to have the energy to NOT sleep at night?! Do it! Sleep when the baby sleeps! Everyone's going to tell you that and they really are right. Most likely though, you'll be like us and use baby's nap time to get a shower, eat, do thank-you notes, check e-mails, return text messages and phone calls and anything else BUT sleep. Hence, you're in Zombie Mama mode because that shut-off switch to "relax" just does not exist in Mama Bears! So sleep already!

It's going to take about a month for the baby to get on any kind of schedule – see our chapter on Scheduling. As such – do not attempt a schedule with your baby in the first weeks at home. The most you can do is help the baby figure out days and nights (this can take at a minimum 2 weeks – which means at 1:00 a.m., your baby thinks it's play time and it's sooo not). We provide tips in the Scheduling chapter when it comes to the nighttime feeds because the more boring and dark you keep the overnight changes and feedings, the more likely baby will figure out nighttime is boring and she might as well sleep vs. party in the nursery woo hoo!!

You know that guy who got your pregnant? Believe it or not, he still loves you even though you've been a bit psycho for almost a year.

And we know you're focusing solely on that little baby you're trying to keep alive and healthy and out of harm's way. But your partner needs some love and attention too. So when your mother offers to come over for a couple hours to watch the baby, go to lunch and get a beer. Or go to the grocery store or a movie with your partner. Yes, you may only talk about the baby, but at least you're doing it while you're looking at your partner instead of standing up and walking over to the baby (or looking down because all you do is hold the baby). More on this in the Marriage chapter.

Your baby is going to cry. Babies cry because they can't talk to you. They cry for your attention, because they're hungry, because they're gassy, because they're tired, because they're lonely. Babies cry because they have the lung capacity to do so. It's the only way they can talk to you. Get used to it. We truly believe mothers inherently know the difference in their babies cries and you learn to tune out the inconsequential "I'm bored – anyone there who wants to pick me up?" cries and the "OHMYGODIFIDON'TGETFEDSOONIMIGHTSTARVETODEATH" cries or the "MOMMYSAVEMEMYSISTERISTRYINGTOSITONMYHEAD" cries. You'll learn too.

In your first month home, don't overdo it. Don't try to be superwoman and schedule a lot of events or think you can do everything you normally do AND care for a newborn. You will need time for your body to heal and you also need to settle into your new family dynamic. It is ok if some of your chores slip or you get behind on responding to emails. Gifts are going to trickle in for the first month or two. Save yourself some insanity and before you've given birth, get some stamps. After the baby arrives, jump onto Walmart.com or some other printing site and print some very simple generic "thank you for your thoughtfulness in celebration of the birth of our son, XYZ." Then when you get a gift, you can send one of those suckers off. Yes it's a bit impersonal but the important thing is that you're thanking the person for the gift, you're including a picture of the baby and then you're done. The last thing you want to do with your awake time is hand-write a lot of thank you notes. KISS, remember?

If this is your second baby that you're bringing home, please consider keeping your first-born in part-time daycare a couple days a week at least to keep their schedule consistent and allow you some bonding time with the new baby without the guilt of "slighting" the first-born. Babies can't remember that you ignored them or held one over the other. A toddler not only remembers but will smear her walls with her poopy diaper in protest.

Hopefully you took advantage of your last month of pregnancy nesting instinct and you made some freezer meals. We know what you're thinking: you're on maternity leave for weeks, home all day with the baby, you'll have plenty of time to cook. No, you won't. You'll be tired and you won't feel like cooking. So make some freezer meals in the last month of pregnancy and then you can pick it up again in the 2nd month home with baby. But the first month of Zombie Mama mode is no time to be using the stove or oven! Need ideas? Go to http://2mamabears.com

Most importantly, in that first month you're home, where you can't spoil the baby with holding her too much, try to enjoy it and soak it all in; your baby is only a newborn once.

Note – households with Pets! You can ask your doctor, check Google, ask friends, but the simplest advice for a house with pets and getting those pets acclimated to baby is to do so BEFORE you bring the baby home. So, have your partner bring a baby's swaddling blanket home from the hospital and let the pet have it – put it on the floor and let them sniff and take it away if they so choose. This gets them used to the baby's scent, plus mom's scent is going to be on there too, so they get a piece of you as well. Don't neglect your fur babies!

Chapter 7: Advice Filtering

The moment you start to tell people you are pregnant, you will start to get advice, whether you want it or not. You will be told every horror story of pregnancy and delivery, whether or not you should circumcise, how vaccinations can lead to autism and 20,000 other facts, fiction and freakish tales. Unfortunately in this day and age of social media and nonstop internet access, you can find answers for everything, topics of conversation you never thought of (you mean there's really an option to NOT circumcise a boy??), and everyone will be quick to share their opinions. Ok, yes, we're doing it here in this book but we're trying to stay away from our opinions and just give you a realistic preview of what's going to happen as well as our approaches for different baby topics that we have found worked.

You'll get unsolicited advice from people in check-out lines, stores and church, from your friends and family members, your neighbors, your co-workers, the nurses at the doctor's office and of course your mother and mother-in-law. You can handle this one of three ways:

1. You can take it all in and get freaked out and do a lot of research and get completely overwhelmed and upset.
2. You can get angry and tell them all to shove their unwanted advice where the sun don't shine, or
3. You can gracefully say "thank you, I'll have to think about that" and then do whatever the hell you want. In the end, it's your pregnancy and your baby and you will decide the best approaches, feeding methods, soothing methods, etc…

Your goal is a healthy happy baby – how you get there is your prerogative.

Along the same lines, you should never feel that you have to defend any decision you've made. It is your body, your circumstances, your home and your child. That being said – your mother successfully raised YOU, right? So chances are, mothers and mothers-in-law might actually know a thing or two. If their suggestion seems way off-base or out of line with what you want to do, still give them a respectful response of "I understand that back in your day you used cloth diapers and found them to be easier on the baby's bottom, but we already work 9 hours a day outside the home and just don't feel that an extra mountain or two of laundry or the expense of a service is the best option for our family." Or "I understand that 'breast is best' but since I'd really like my partner to be a part of the early feeding process, so we're just going to use bottles – my pediatrician has recommended a great formula that is quite similar to the nutrients in breast milk so we feel confident our decision is best for our baby and for ourselves." Just know those close to you mean well and just want to help. Appreciate them. They mean well. Those not close to you need to shove off.

Chapter 8: Let's Talk Schedule

Experts can't seem to agree on whether you really need to put your baby on a schedule or, if you do schedule, at what age to start. We think everyone can agree that children benefit and thrive on a schedule, knowing when things will happen at certain times, sort of like school – but that's years down the road, so why worry now with the baby?

The answer to that question, you start now in the infant stage because you enjoy your sanity. You enjoy knowing that you can go to the grocery store with the baby and have 99.9% probability of no melt-downs due to feeding times or nap time infringement. We're going to provide some example schedules with a couple caveats – one, not everything works for every baby, so modify as needed. Two, just when you have a schedule mastered, something will change and you'll have to amend it, so be flexible. We also believe that a full baby = happy baby = easier to schedule so it's not just a feeding schedule but a sleep schedule as well, with plenty of activity to ensure that nap is taken! If you happen to have a non-napper AND the baby is content at all times – great! But most people see a definite shift in demeanor if the baby misses a nap, cuts a nap short or doesn't get to bed on time; the happy baby is quickly replaced with tired, zombie, monster baby.

The best you can manage in that first month home with baby is two things – straightening out days and nights and getting baby on a feeding schedule. Sleep is still going to be a bit out of whack but you might be able to set forth a bit of a routine anyways, if you can stick to a feeding schedule.

Breastfeeding – Best Told by Kim

Making the decision to breastfeed your baby is a BIG decision and one that only you can make. There are gobs of studies out there that will tell you all the reasons why you should, but you still have to decide if it is the best thing for you AND your family. It involves a family decision because it really does take commitment from everyone in your household because everyone is impacted, not just you and the baby.

I decided that I would breastfeed Allyssa, my oldest. I had no idea what that really meant or entailed, I just knew a bunch of my friends who were also new mamas were doing it and I heard it was the best thing for the baby. Ok, sounds great, let's do this! Well, Allyssa was born tongue tied. I had never even heard of tongue tie, nor had any idea what it had to do with this baby latching properly. Well, it had everything to do with it. Allyssa's tongue tie was not found until she was almost 6 weeks old and we couldn't get it corrected by a specialist until she was 8 weeks old. Allyssa and I had spent the first 6 weeks of her life crying; yes, **both** of us. She was literally starving because she could not latch properly and therefore was not able to get enough milk. Hence the crying. As a first time mama, this was extremely stressful. So, when the doctor told me I had to start supplementing with formula so she would start gaining weight, I stopped breastfeeding. I figured, why put in all this effort if I have to give her formula anyhow.

I am telling you this somewhat of a horror story to make what I consider to be my most significant point on this topic. If you decided to breastfeed, you need to get educated BEFORE the baby arrives. You will hear that it is the most natural thing in the world. It may very well be, but it doesn't come naturally to a first time mama unless you have had some education. There is a ton of literature, books, and most hospitals offer educational classes at a very cheap rate. I encourage you to get educated.

So, before Addalyn, my middle daughter was born, I took a class through the hospital where I planned to deliver the baby. The classes are lead by Lactation Consultants, who are also RN's. Mainly, I took the class to ease my anxiety because I did not want a repeat performance of what I experienced with Allyssa. The class helped tremendously. I had clear expectations, a plan to follow, and a slew of resources to call on if I needed help along the way. This made all the difference. I breastfed Addalyn until she was 13 months old and never had any issues. I did have her tongue checked in the hospital, and it was also tied, but it was clipped before we were discharged. I learned that tongue tie is hereditary...Aubree, my 5 month old, was also tongue tied!

Scheduling is very similar with breastfeeding as bottle feeding. The biggest difference is that when the baby is nursing, you really don't know exactly how much they are drinking.

Admittedly, I am not a scheduler to the degree Amanda is, but, I do still schedule. The first month with a newborn is not much different for a breastfeeding or bottle feeding mama. You are still in zombie mode and the baby seems to want to eat around the clock. The experts will tell you to feed the baby on demand, meaning when the baby is hungry, you feed them.

After the first month, the goal is to stretch the feedings out a bit and start working towards the baby sleeping a longer stretch at night. I have been super blessed with Aubree as she has been sleeping at least 6 hours since she was 3 weeks old. My goal was to feed her every 3 hours except at night. She wakes up at 6am, so I feed her immediately upon waking. She eats again at 9am, 12pm, 3pm, 6pm, and 9pm.

As I am writing this, she is 5 months old, and she is still on this same schedule except we have introduced cereal at her 9am, 3pm, and 6pm feedings.

If you are going back to work, you will also need to plan a pumping schedule. You will need to start pumping while you are still on maternity leave to build up a supply of milk in your freezer for when you return to work. Please make sure you review the guidelines on how long you can keep expressed milk at room temperature, in a fridge, freezer, and deep freeze. This will ensure you have plenty of milk while you are away from the baby. It is also helpful to have if you want to have any kind of a social life! Remember that guy you're married to? I bet he would love to have a night out without a baby attached to your boob!

Most experts will tell you to start pumping after your baby has reached a month old. It is best to let the baby stimulate a good supply of milk before you start pumping. The single most important thing I can tell you, breastfeeding is supply and demand. Your body will make whatever amount it needs to cover the demand.

I had a simple pumping schedule while I was on maternity leave. I wanted to keep it as minimal as possible so I could maximize my time with the baby and the rest of my family. When Aubree reached a month old, I started nursing her on one side for her initial feeding of the day and I would pump the other side. I did this for several reasons:

1. You have the most milk first thing in the morning.
2. We were always at home at that time of day.
3. It increased my milk supply because she would demand more from one side and then I would pump the other.
4. After I was done pumping, I didn't have to worry about it for the remainder of the day.

Now that I am back to work, I pump at 10am and 2pm every day. You body will adjust to being away from the baby. Some mamas follow their baby's eating schedule and pump at the same times their baby is or would be eating. That is not practical for me at work and my body adjusted so I still get the same amount of milk. Please note, the first few days you are away from your baby, your body will be adjusting and you will pump a lot more milk than the baby takes in a bottle. Breastfed babies don't drink nearly as much as from a bottle as formula-fed babies. The most both of my breastfed girls have ever taken from a bottle is 4 ounces. The theory is, they prefer to nurse from mama, so they will drink enough to hold them over until they can be with you again. So, don't be alarmed. They will chunk up just the same! As a matter of fact, my Aubree and Amanda's Emma are one day apart. Aubree is breastfed, Emma has been formula-fed and they are almost identical in both length and weight!

BOTTLE FEEDING

Again – how you feed your baby is a conversation with yourself, your partner and your pediatrician. Also remember – you may want to breastfed but extenuating circumstances (infection, lack of milk production, undiagnosed tongue tie) may mean you have to formula feed. Don't beat yourself up over it – what is most important is that your baby is getting enough to eat!

With formula feeding, it's a bit easier to institute a feeding schedule earlier and with some success, because

> 1. Anyone can give the baby a bottle, if you happen to be napping and
> 2. You know exactly how much the baby is getting.

If you can, start the baby on a feeding schedule in the hospital. Both of Amanda's girls were on a feed every three hours schedule by the time they got home with little variation. Emma turned out to be a projectile vomiter and was losing weight (she was also three weeks early so I blame an under-developed stomach), which meant we had to feed her more often and a special cereal-fortified formula for about 2 months but then she bulked up, her stomach matured and we went back to our usual formula from Sam's Club.

The rule of thumb on bottle feeding is going to be 2 ½ ounces for every POUND that the baby weighs each day. So if your baby is 6 pounds, he should be taking around 15 ounces a day. Some babies are just skimpy eaters and some are big eaters, so again, schedules and feeding amounts need to be adjusted to your baby. When you need to make any change to the schedule – whether it be ounces or timing, do it in increments – and we're talking 10 minute and ½ ounce increments. It usually takes about 3 to 5 days to set a new routine so it also takes patience!

Talk to your pediatrician if you have any concerns.

Some pediatricians and experts will tell you that a baby HAS to feed every two to three hours and if baby is sleeping, wake him up and feed him. We'd like to tell those jerks to pound dirt because we prescribed to a do not wake a sleeping baby philosophy and our kids still thrived. Get the baby scheduled correctly and know that it takes a miracle for the baby to "sleep through" a feeding anyways because babies get hungry, just like us!

Here's a sample weekly schedule for a "typical" newborn:

Week 1	2 oz of formula every 3 hours – diaper change BEFORE each bottle
Week 2	3 oz of formula every 3 ½ hours
Week 3	4 oz of formula every 3 ½ to 4 hours
Week 4	4 ½ to 5 oz of formula every 4 hours
Week 5	5 to 5 ½ oz of formula every 4 hours
Week 6	5 ½ to 6 ½ oz of formula every 4 hours
Week 7	6 ½ oz of formula every 4 hours

So basically, after two weeks, you should essentially be feeding baby at midnight, 4 a.m., 8 a.m., Noon, 4 p.m., 8 p.m., Midnight. At least you know for that time period you should be able to sleep 7 hours (take away half an hour for the Midnight and 4 a.m. change & feed time). Not bad really!

Let's talk about those nighttime feedings and helping the baby figure out days and nights – anything after 8 p.m. and before, say, 6 a.m. Avoid Amanda's mistake of turning on all the lights, talking to the baby, smiling with the baby and making it fun time for the baby. All that does it tell the baby – "hey! It's awake time and I want to spend it with Mama!" and then you're up for an hour trying to get the baby back to sleep. Instead, only use the light of a nightlight, dim lamp or hallway light (Amanda's daughter was born in December and had an electric candle in the window – perfect! She didn't take it down until the baby was going through the night). If bottle feeding, don't go into the baby's room until you have the bottle with you – go in prepared! Get the baby and quietly soothe him while you change his diaper and then sit down to feed him. Keep it as quiet and dull and dark as possible and the baby will quickly learn that waking up at night is just boring and they'll just go back to sleep as they're feeding or shortly thereafter.

DO NOT TALK TO THE BABY! Seriously – it sucks, but if you want the baby to sleep longer at night, you have to make the night feedings dull.

By the end of the first month, you'll be ready for some real sleep and baby will be too. All you want to do at the start of that 5th week is stretch the baby through the night a little bit. Try holding back some of the formula at the 4 p.m. feeding to be able to add more to the bedtime bottle. You might be able to start coaxing ½ an ounce more into the bedtime feeding – you'll just have to see what works for the baby. You'll want to make sure you have a good absorbent diaper on the baby too – half the reason they wake up is because they're wet. Most of the name-brand diapers have 12-hour or "overnight" diapers, though the sizes might not start until size 2. They do run smaller, though, so don't be afraid to try them early on!

In Week 5, try to push the last feeding, your 8 p.m. from the schedule, to 9 p.m. and make that a big bottle. Between a full belly and a good absorbent diaper, your baby should be able to go beyond the four hour mark, even up to six hours, before the next feeding and diaper change. Make that overnight bottle ½ oz to 1 oz larger than normal and again, you should get an extra hour from the baby until morning. It may only happen in 15 minute increments over the course of that week, but the baby should be getting used to a longer stretch between just those overnight feedings and sleep better. You'll continue that pattern until you see that the baby is able to sleep from that 9 p.m. feeding to around 4 a.m. – basically, you're eliminating that midnight to 2 a.m. feeding! It might take a couple weeks, but it will happen.

By 8 weeks old, your baby should be up to about 6 to 8 ounces of formula at every feeding, no less than 6 ounces. Your baby won't sleep through the night until he's consuming around 32 ounces of formula a day. What you'll be trying to do between weeks 8 and 12 is push the baby's bedtime back to an earlier time (who wants a toddler up at 9 p.m.?) and pushing that wake-up time to something more reasonable and conducive to your own schedule, especially if you're going back to work.

That brings up a good point – when you're setting the baby's schedule, if you're going back to work, you need to work towards THAT schedule, not the easier one of maternity leave. Think about what time you need to leave for work. How long does it take you to get ready for work? How long does it take the baby to eat? Work your way backwards to determine the best time for baby to wake up.

It's a fact of life that when you get the baby on a schedule and he has it mastered, something will change it. The baby will get sick, start teething or just change his wake-up time. So be prepared to adjust. Samantha is on her 3rd schedule in 6 months and it's just because she's evolving. And don't forget about those daylight savings time zones! We give guidance on the blog for this fun time of your life, twice a year!

What follows are the schedules that worked for Amanda and her sitters, for various ages within the first year.

Bottle only (months two through four) – Remember, after month one, you're working on eliminating that midnight feeding and stretching baby through the night, so Amanda actually had two schedules by 8 weeks that she would follow – one if the baby woke up at 3:30 a.m., one if she went through to 6 a.m.

TIME	BABY GETS	NOTES
3:30 a.m.	4 oz formula	Feed & back to bed
7:45 a.m.	8 oz formula	@ the Sitter's
morning		She'll have some activity time and usually down for a nap by 9:30, up around 11:30
NOON	7 oz formula	
afternoon		She'll have some activity time and usually down for a nap by 2:00, up around 4:00
4:00 p.m.	7 oz formula	
5:15 p.m.	Picked up from sitter	
5:30 p.m.	4 oz formula	
evening		She liked to snooze between 7 & 8 – we'd let her sleep in the swing, wake her up, change her, bit of a bottle & back down for bed
8:00 p.m.	6 oz formula @ Bedtime	Bedtime

TIME	BABY GETS	BABY DOES
6:00 a.m.	8 oz formula	
morning		She'll have some activity time and usually down for a nap by 7:30, up around 9:30
10:00 a.m.	8 oz formula	

afternoon		She'll have some activity time and usually down for a nap by 11:30, up around 1:30
2:00 p.m.	8 oz formula	
6:00 p.m.	6 oz formula	
evening		She liked to snooze between 7 & 8 – we'd let her sleep in the swing, wake her up, change her, bit of a bottle & back down for bed
8:00 p.m.	6 oz formula @ Bedtime	Bedtime

The schedules above worked to at least get Amanda and her husband out the door and through the workdays but eventually, it started to feel like all Samantha was doing was eating and then napping when she felt like it. Thankfully, sanity arrived in the advice of her sister and the schedule below was implemented. It only eliminated the making of one bottle every day, but it felt like it completely improved their lives and set Samantha to a clock on her naps. Any non-nap time is play time or reading time, whether it's by herself on a play mat in her pre-sitting days or in a playpen now. Amanda insisted that Samantha learn independent play so she could entertain herself rather than need 24/7 attention from sitters or her parents.

Bottle & Baby Food and Sippy Cup (months 4 through 8) **By the time they are really eating and using a sippy cup, you can eliminate bottles if they are drinking enough through the cups. We kept Samantha on a bedtime bottle until she turned 1.

TIME	BABY GETS	NOTES
6:30 a.m.	Cereal w/ fruit, 2 oz formula	If at home, start an 8oz bottle to finish by 8 a.m. – if going to sitter, give her 2 oz and sitter will give her a 6 oz bottle made there
7:45 a.m.	Finish bottle	
8:30 a.m.		NAP - she may get an hour and a half to almost 2 hours
11:00 a.m.	Start her lunch	4 oz of food (1/2 veg, 1/2 fruit/yogurt) & start 7 oz bottle
12:00 p.m.	Finish her bottle - about 6 oz	
1:15 p.m.		Down for a nap, about 2 hours
3:00 p.m.	6 oz formula	
6:00 p.m.	Start her Dinner	4 oz food (1/2 veg, 1/2 fruit/yogurt) & start 8 oz bottle
7:00 p.m.	Finish off the dinner bottle	Bedtime

The amounts of food may change, but the basic schedule is unchanged EVERY DAY. That is your lifeline – you can change amounts, the baby may sleep more or less on any given day, but meals and naps/downtimes are the same and you have to keep it consistent.

Chapter 9: Soothing the Baby

There are 1,000 different ways to soothe your baby – Google them and you'll see. Once you've covered three basics of baby: food, sleep & diaper, your next step is to figure out how to soothe the baby. When he's startled, scared, annoyed, pissed off because someone looked at him wrong, doesn't have your immediate attention or any other reason that we can't comprehend because, well, babies can't talk.

Depending on the baby gear you've purchased/received, you will want to try the following to see if you can soothe the baby. Your methods of soothing are going to fall into some general categories: Motion, Comfort, Swaddling, Noise, Gas or Colic, and I have no idea…so what do I do now?!

Motion: Think back to when you were pregnant – that newborn was nice and warm and being rocked all day long! So doesn't it make sense that some motion might be nice right about now? This is where a rocking chair or rocking recliner, stationary swing, bouncer with vibration, walking the baby or even just sitting and rocking/swaying the baby in your arms could be your salvation. When desperate, go for a car ride!

Comfort: Check the baby's clothing and any straps if the baby is strapped into anything – maybe there's a tag or strap irritating her. Look for irritating hairs from you, the sitter, etc… that may have wrapped around baby's finger, become caught between a onesie and their skin, etc.. Make sure the baby is nice and warm but not too warm (good luck finding the happy medium, just remember layers are your friend). Is there a slight breeze from an open window or A/C vent that's hitting them and giving them a chill? Their skin is very sensitive in the beginning and just the slightest discomfort can lead to uncontrollable crying. Sometimes the baby just wants held if she's in the swing or sometimes the baby is being held and she now wants the swing!

Swaddling: Dr. Harvey Karp really is a genius and we both highly recommend you check out Happiest Baby on the Block and all of his theories. But his Five S's are ingenious, simple and really effective for most babies. Swaddle, Side/Stomach position, Shush, Swing, Suck (binkie). Swaddling is the key – we've recommended the Miracle Blanket, and you'll want to know how to swaddle with just a large receiving blanket as well. Let's go back to the womb – baby was not only getting rocked and nice and warm, but he was also confined – the sudden freedom after he's born isn't freeing, it's actually completely foreign and unappreciated and that baby just wants to be closed up, held close and kept warm. Swaddling does just that.

Noise: In addition to all the other comforts of your belly, the baby also had the constant noise of your heartbeat and other noises he could hear. Complete silence is NOT your baby's friend. That's why we recommend a noise machine for the nursery and why all the soothing toys of bouncers, swings, etc… all come with white noise, water noise and music options – because babies are used to noise!

Gas or Colic: If your baby has colic or gas, it's a bit tougher. There are Over-The-Counter (OTC) gas drops you can give the baby or try about an ounce of really warm water in a bottle, bicycle-pump their legs, pushing their legs into their bellies to push out that gas, belly massage, or laying them on your knees, stomach down, and bouncing them a bit to push out the gas.

How do you know if it's colic? If your baby is crying inconsolably (meaning all other soothing methods have failed) for three hours or more every day, it could be colic. If you're breastfeeding, you might want to cut some irritants out of your diet such as caffeine, onions, dairy and other foods that could be irritating the baby. If you're formula feeding, you might want to consider switching formula brands or to a gentle formula that helps with gas and reflex. Dr. Brown's bottles are specially designed to reduce reflux and gas with feedings.

I have no idea so what do I do now?! Remember – sometimes babies just cry. They're angry, tired, or just can't express themselves in any other way. Your motherly instinct will kick in and you'll know if it's just a fussy time or gas or if you should wonder if something more serious is wrong. And yes – Motherly Instinct does in fact exist – we can't really explain it other than, we believe there is a basic human instinct that just *tells* you what to do!

As always – when in doubt, call the doctor. When you reach a breaking point and you just don't know if you can take another minute, you call in reinforcements and walk away from the baby. Give yourself a break and it should go without saying, never, ever, shake a baby. We all reach that point of "oh my god, I'd shove you back up inside me if it meant not hearing you cry for another minute" and that's when you need to put the baby down and walk outside for five minutes. Or call your mother or sister-in-law and say you need a break, can she please come sit with the screamer while you do anything BUT listen to the baby cry. Call for help!!

Chapter 10: Feeding Baby – Solid Foods

You have to make the decision to breastfeed before the baby gets here (and remember, you can make all the plans you want but sometimes, mother nature has different plans). You need to know what you want to do because within about an hour of that baby surfacing from your vag, it's feeding time! We've also talked about the recommendations if you're bottle feeding, to be sure to try to feed your infant 2 ½ ounces for every pound of body weight each day, and you can increase the amount by half an ounce as you see the baby is taking a full bottle and seems to want more.

If you are bottle feeding, your pediatrician, whom you've met before you had the baby and informed that you either want to breastfeed or bottle feed, might recommend a particular brand. Also, feel free to ask the hospital what brand it typically uses because if the baby does well on it, that might be the brand you want to use. For instance, Amanda knew that her husband Doug was a baby who spit up constantly and to this day, her husband has serious heartburn and acid reflux issues. She assumed her daughter could inherit those tendencies, and a couple friends had recommended Enfamil Sensitive formula. She ran that suggestion by both her OB/GYN and her selected pediatrician and got an all-clear. It happened that the hospital also used Enfamil newborn formula, so there was no switching of a brand. At two weeks, she introduced her daughter to the Sam's brand of Gentlease formula with the same ingredients and percentages as Enfamil and has had no issues.

Sometimes, though, your child might have issues so be prepared to possibly switch formulas if your baby has problems. There are also instances of some mothers not producing enough milk when breastfeeding so they have to supplement with formula. We know you may have a plan, but again, please be flexible and remember the health of your child outweighs your personal desires. Get used to it – your child is now first for everything in your life.

Prior to 2012, the AAP recommended that all infants be introduced to pureed solid foods between the ages of four and six months. Now the guidelines have been revised to a minimum of 6 months of age, when the child can hold his head up independently, his body has had a chance to develop the proper gut bacteria to properly digest food and the developed gag reflex to avoid choking. Signs that your baby is ready for solid foods includes putting his hands in his mouth, making chewing motions with his mouth, reaching for food on your own plate, being able to take food off a fork or spoon and not closing his mouth when food is offered.

There are even more options for baby food once your baby is old enough to start having it. Your pediatrician will provide guidance on when you should start introducing baby cereal and strained fruits and veggies. Remember – everything is a guideline and your baby will often times give you clues that he's ready for something more. Plus – every single baby progresses at different paces, even among siblings!

If you are overwhelmed by the options for formula, there are even more options and brands for baby food, so brace yourself:

- Homemade – more and more, mamas are opting to make their own baby food so they can save money and know exactly what is going in their little one's mouth
- Organic store-bought – with all the debate on processed foods, many mamas are choosing to buy organic. There does tend to be more variety in the types of foods offered with organic, in our opinion.
- Mainstream store- bought - this is the traditional (Gerber) baby food we were almost all raised on!

Your decision of whether to make your own or buy it is up to you – remember, babies are only on baby food for a few months, depending on when you start them and when they start getting their teeth and can chew more textures. Amanda's daughter actually started refusing baby cereal around 7 ½ months of age after loving it for months – she then started making baby cereal pancakes that her daughter could chew and she loved them! A pancake and ½ a container of yogurt was her 9 month old daughter's standard breakfast. When you do start the baby on baby food, you still continue with formula – the food doesn't really provide them the nutrients that formula or breast milk does, at this point. So baby should still be taking in around 30 ounces of formula or breast milk a day along with around two to four ounces of food at each feeding.

We shouldn't have to but we will add the occasional note of your child may eat more or less than the guidelines – that's why they're guidelines and you need to adjust according to your child's needs.

Even more fun is when your child will eat something one day and then the next time you give it to him, he refuses to eat it. Think of it this way – YOU, as an adult, get to choose what you eat – your baby does not. And some days, grilled cheese just isn't as appetizing as a hot dog or scrambled egg. However, you don't want to get in the habit of making four different dinners either so keep it reasonable for your sanity's sake. The habits you start when they are 8 months old will continue when they are 2 years old if you aren't careful. Samantha gets 2 chances at a dinner option on a "feeling generous" night if Amanda so chooses. If she rejects meal option two, it's extra of something else she is eating (she gets a fruit/yogurt, veggie and protein with every meal) and then it's a guaranteed full bottle before bed time. The kid isn't going to starve if she skips her grilled cheese one night.

There are some foods the pose certain health or allergy risks and we want to make you aware of these so that you can follow your own pediatrician's guidelines and discuss these with your care provider.

These guidelines are from the AAP (American Academy of Pediatrics).

FOOD	WHY	WHEN
Honey	May cause botulism in infants under 1 year	After 1 year of age
Peanut Butter	Potential Allergen	After 6 months to 2 years of age
(Tree) Nuts	Potential Allergen & Choking Hazard	After 6 months to 2 years of age
Citrus or Acidic Fruits	May cause a rash but not necessarily an allergen	After 6 months to 1 year of age
Raw Strawberries, Raspberries, Blackberries	Potential Allergen	After 6 months to 1 year of age
Corn	Potential Allergen	After 6 months to 1 year of age
Egg Whites	Potential Allergen	After 6 months to 1 year of age
Whole (Vitamin D) Milk	Potential Allergen & Digestive issues	After 1 year of age
Wheat	Potential Allergen	After 6 months to 1 year of age
Grapes	Choking Hazard	After 10 months or 1 year of age
Shellfish	Potential Allergen	After 6 months to 1 year of age

Chapter 11: Milestones

Especially as a first-time Mom, and perhaps with each additional child, you may be a bit neurotic about what your baby should be doing when at what point in their development. Let's go back to every pregnancy is different, every baby is different, every home is different – are you getting us yet? Every kid is different – so please treat milestones as *guidelines* and not absolutes! If you have a genuine concern about the development of your child or lack thereof, talk to your pediatrician.

Month 1: Generally, this is a blurry time for both of you – you're a mommy zombie and baby is trying to figure out why it's so bright out and why she isn't constantly moving and rocking like she used to be in your belly. She can't see more than 8 to 12 inches away (pretty much the distance it takes to gaze at you while you feed or hold her) and will be drawn to black and white images. Her hearing is fully developed, though, and certain sounds, such as your voice or your husband's, may cause her to turn her head towards them when she hears them.

It's our opinion that the first couple of months of a child, if not the first three, are like the fourth trimester and that baby wants held, rocked and comforted and you are free to do so to your heart's content. You can't spoil a newborn at this point (aside maybe from rocking to sleep every night). So hold your baby as she starts to lift and turn her head herself and learns what her fists are.

Your pediatrician will be asking about certain milestones at your well-check's, to look for warning signs such as baby not feeding or sucking well, not focusing his eyes or watching things move that are nearby, reacting to bright lights and loud sounds.

Month 3: By now, baby is smiling and it's not just gas! The more you interact with him and give him play time, the more interactive he becomes – congratulations, you now feel like you actually have a baby and not an inert crying/pooping/feeding machine! Tummy time, which you should have started fairly early in the process (some start at a few weeks but definitely by month 2 to avoid flat head if nothing else, but also to strengthen that neck!), should be a daily occurrence and baby should be able to lift his head and chest, almost like a push-up. This will set the stage for rolling over – something you'll celebrate at first and then soon dread because it takes some time before they learn how to flip back over! By three months, he should also be able to recognize Mommy from across the room.

Months 4 through 7: Your baby is now fully engaged with you and the rest of the world! She should be smiling, babbling and laughing on a regular basis. By 6 months she should be eating solid foods and by 7 months she should be rolling back and forth from her back to tummy to her back again, sitting up without help and jumping up and down on your lap while you hold her. She may also be perfecting her raking grasp to pull objects, and food, closer to her. The world is a full-colored one and she'll love looking in mirrors and playing peek-a-boo. She may be starting to crawl so be prepared to either baby proof and put up safety gates at all stairs or else putting up a play-yard in your living room to keep the baby contained and safe while she starts to explore her new abilities and perfects the art of independent play.

Months 8 through 12: Baby's on the go! Crawling and maybe even walking, he's getting around quickly. He can sit on his own and pull himself up onto anything, it seems! His babbling may start to sound more like words – usually mama and dada are the first recognizable phrases because they're the easiest to pronounce. Various hand gestures to indicate what baby wants, and doesn't want, become a prevalent part of your life. He may be able to drink from a sippy or straw cup now and pretend to talk on the phone or have conversations with his stuffed animals. It may also be that your once extremely sociable baby is now a hesitant toddler when it comes to strangers or family members he doesn't see regularly. We call it the stranger danger phase. He just needs to become comfortable with that person again, which may take a few minutes of play while you hold him or a few continuous visits. Just don't force the interaction, it's a natural phase for the child to go through. Separation anxiety is normal and may occur when you drop him off at day care too – this too shall pass!

At your child's 1 year check up, your pediatrician will be looking for some developmental warning signs, such as if your baby isn't yet crawling, drags to one side when she does crawl, can't stand with support, doesn't say any words or doesn't use any gestures with her hands or shakes her head for no and pointing.

Remember that guy who got you pregnant and held your hair back as you puked in the toilet during your first trimester? And the person who rubbed your disgusting swollen "cankles" in your last trimester? And that partner who almost lost a finger due to you squeezing their hand to hard in the delivery room and whispered "I love you – you're amazing" after your child was born?

You know that marriage or partnership or whatever you want to call it you have going on in which you are two adults trying to raise and not permanently damage that little person who came screaming out of your vagina (or belly)? We know that you are absolutely in love with that child you have created, that you are 100% focused on that baby, the schedule, keeping some semblance of a clean house, figuring out what in the hell the baby needs at 3:00 a.m. and trying to wash your hair at least once a week and put on clean underwear almost daily, but there's just one more thing, Mama. You gotta keep the LOVE alive.

You're both tired. You're both stressed. We get it – in about 6 months, things are going to feel normal. But you don't have six months. At your six week check-up, your OB/GYN will give you the green light to make some magic, get some booty, do the deed, dance the horizontal mambo. And you're going to be scared shitless. Your husband will be panting in anticipation of finally being with his wife again. You're going to wonder if you're ever going to want that baby maker near your body, let alone in that same tunnel of love your baby tried to destroy.

Think of it as, well, basically losing your virginity. The first time was awkward, probably a bit painful, and you kinda just wanted it to end already so you could say you did it because everyone swore it gets better with every time. Well, this does too. You might want some lubrication to keep things going smoothly. Maybe a glass of wine or two. Some nice mood music and lighting would help too – as would a sleeping baby. Being intimate with your partner was a big part of your life before baby, remember? This is something that helps keep you guys connected and brings you back to feeling like there's a life outside of poopy diapers and burp cloths.

Your partner may go back to work a week after the baby is born. Your days will be spent in the same routine with a non-speaking house-mate while your husband gets to go to the office, have adult conversations, power lunches and not get covered in baby puke. Don't get annoyed if your husband doesn't pay a lot of attention to your play-by-play of your day.

Especially with your first baby, the thought of leaving that little bundle of joy for more than an hour to run to the store is just heart breaking. We PROMISE you that the baby won't be traumatized by you having a date night, going to dinner (actually we always did lunch, we were too tired for evening dates!) or a movie or IKEA without toting the baby along with you. When you have a date night, please try very hard to NOT text the babysitter 20 times, don't talk about the baby and the color of his poop today. Talk about LIFE. You know, that thing you used to have BEFORE you gave birth to the football you dote on every hour of every day.

For some of us, there is no decision – we're a two-income household so going back to work is a given. For others, once you factor in the daycare payments, price of formula or time to pump breast milk, etc… you're better off staying at home or working a swing shift, part-time, etc… It's not an easy decision either way, believe it or not. For those Mama's who decide to stay home, they may feel that they are "giving up" their careers or "wasting" their college educations, decreasing their future marketability and thus jeopardizing their future re-employment. There's the wonderment of "what will I do all day" and can you really afford to lose that income? For Mama's choosing to go back to work, there's the ever-familiar guilt of leaving your child with *gasp* a stranger!

Ok we're dramatizing a bit here but still, someone who did NOT give birth to your child will be, like it or not, spending more time with your child than you will except for weekends. Feel like shit yet? It's ok, we all do. But if you start early (Amanda reserved her sitter when she was 3 months pregnant) and do your research and meet the caregivers, hopefully by the time you actually return to work, you at least have faith in the loving, competent care your child will receive in your absence.

And we promise – no matter what anyone says, your child will NOT mistake the sitter for you, her mother. She will never PREFER the sitter over you (unless maybe you're disciplining her) and she will NEVER have any doubt that you are the person who gave her life and the sitter or daycare is where she goes to play with all those strange kids until someone comes to get her. Really.

We think a lot of women have a great misconception about what it means to be a stay-at-home mom. As in they don't have to "work." Well, here's a newsflash for ya – you may THINK that maternity leave is a kickback and relax with the baby time of your life, but it actually can get pretty spastic as you TRY to channel your inner-June Cleaver and do the laundry, bake some cookies, make dinner every night, keep the house clean, keep yourself clean, help the kids with homework, weed the flower beds, do the grocery shopping, reorganize the closets, kill the dust-bunnies, water the plants, clean out the refrigerator, make the beds, iron your husband's shirts so you don't have to buy new ones when he burns holes in them from the iron and clean the kitty litter box and/or pick up the dog's poop bombs in the yard. Mom's who stay at home WORK – they just aren't PAID for that work with money.

You have to make the decision on 1. What will work for your household income and 2. What will work for YOU. As much as I would LOVE to be home every day, I still don't think I'd want the kids home WITH ME every day. A little break, a little sanity, is always a good thing! So I use my big-girl job as my sanity check and then hightail it out of here at 5pm every day to get home with my babies. I think either role will force you to become more efficient, multi-faceted and give you a sense of value and a great example for your children. Now – if you become one of those bon bon-eating, soap-watching, maids do everything for you, nanny has the kids so you can do yoga and pilates 4 hours a day kind of stay-at-home moms, well, we don't like you.

Chapter 14: Going Back to Work

Yes it sucks but we have some tips to keep it manageable – you might want to turn this section over to your husband/partner because they're going to have to step up their game!

The first two weeks of going back to work suck in every way possible. No matter how much you plan, do practice runs, set alarms and pack your lunches, it will result in absolutely manic mornings and chaotic evenings, while you spend all day trying to stay awake and drink twice the amount of caffeine you normally would. This too shall pass. Some tips to help you get into a routine (notice, routine, schedule – key parts of our days!)

1. Daddy has to help. Yes, you are Super Mom! Yes, you feed the baby a bottle faster, leap over laundry baskets, dress the baby cuter, cut the pancakes better and tie their shoes better. But daddy can do it too and he should. Make sure he's up and helping. If he keeps hitting snooze, put a baby with a poopy diaper on his chest facing his mouth – gets him up every time.

2. Your baby will take the slowest bottle in the morning. Probably not, but it will feel like it, so please, do yourself and your sanity a favor and plan on half an hour to feed the baby in the mornings. If it only takes 15 minutes, great! You get to put on makeup today.

3. Once your baby is on baby food, but before finger foods, do yourself and their clothes a favor and don't get them dressed until AFTER breakfast. No matter how many bibs you use, the food goes everywhere and it's easier to change out of a sleeper than pull something else off and then back over their heads for some reason. Amanda didn't let Samantha start eating breakfast in her human clothes until she was almost a year old!

4. Pack your bags – lunch bags, computer bags, diaper bags, purse, workout bag, whatever – the night before. Put anything you can in the car in the evening if possible or at least have it right at the garage door so Daddy can take a trip or two in the mornings. Envision yourself carrying your coffee, a toddler, your purse, your computer bag, your lunch bag down the stairs to the garage. Yes it's possible, but how much do you trust the toddler you're carrying with the hot coffee SHE's carrying to help you out?

5. KISS – breakfast needs to be simple. Chances are, the sitter or daycare is going to do a snack the minute your munchkin

walks in. Why? Because food pacifies. So you are probably safe with just a waffle or pancake (make your own and freeze them, then toast them – see recipe on the http://2mamabears.com blog) and some fruit because the kid will be eating a second breakfast in about an hour. So don't get hung up on the food pyramid, just get some food in the kid!

6. What time do you need to get out the door? 7:30? Then start packing up at 7:20. Even with all the pre-packing, it really will take 10 minutes to get coats on, baby carriers fastened and toddler's fastened into carseats. Every time.

7. Mama – if you are picking up the angel from daycare or the sitter, do yourself a favor and bring or wear flats/flip flops/snow boots to change into. Your sitter has been caring for kids all day, the walk is not going to be shoveled. You want to dare 4 inch heels in the pouring down rain, have at it, but adding a lopsided 25 pound baby carrier with a baby loaded in it is not a fun workout.

8. Dinnertime – well, good luck. The crockpot is your friend. Remember – your sanity saver is that schedule you've put the baby on, but especially once you're on food, dinner comes early and so does a 7pm bedtime!

Chapter 15: Mommy's Guilt

We don't believe in it. Neither should you. If you are doing everything you can do keep the house running, your career going, the kids fed, bathed, happy, your marriage successful, then be happy! Or at least toss the guilt! We have to stop comparing ourselves to other moms. We can't feel guilty because we don't make it to every ball practice, classroom play or monitor lunches. If your kid falls down, it's not your fault.

For some reason, and maybe it's always been this way, but some moms feel the need to compete on every level with other moms. Best lunch monitor mom, best soccer mom, best cookie mom, best snuggling mom, best whatever is going on mom. We all strive for the best, and then quickly become satisfied with survival.

Whether you're a working mom or a mom of more than one child, you're not going to be able to go to every single "donut with mommy" day, Grades 2 through 4 ensemble production of Noah's Ark or every soccer practice. Nor should you feel guilty about it. Because the reason that the kids have the soccer uniform, school activities and everything else in their life is because their parents provide for it, one way or another. The kids will get that. Like it or not, they'll learn about priorities at an early age and that sometimes, you just have to choose. You can't be in two places at once. So throw that guilt out. Your kids will screw up and it's not (always) a reflection on you. Raise your kids right, teach them some morals and then cross your fingers on a daily basis that something sunk into their heads and that they don't become social misfits.

Chapter 16: Your Body After Baby

One of the first things you want after the baby arrives is your old body back! You leave the hospital still looking pregnant (sorry to burst THAT bubble) because, well, you just expelled that infant 3 days ago – your body doesn't suddenly shrivel everything back up – it takes time! It's not going to happen overnight. You may not be cleared for physical exercise up to 6 weeks after delivery. After a c-section, you're not even allowed to lift anything heavier than the baby or drive your car!

That being said – let's be real for a minute. You uterus has just been stretched out to the size of a small car. Your breasts have engorged themselves to the size of cantaloupes. And while we ALL hope that EVERYTHING will shrink back to its original state….that's not always the case.

Amanda wore a size 8 shoe for the first 38 years of her life….two pregnancies and swollen feet later, she's now a size 8 ½. Yes, even your feet may "grow" and never be back to your pre-pregnancy size. Don't toss those shoes just yet, just be prepared for some shifts and changes, that may or may not go back to original sizes!

The good news? Giving birth immediately takes around 10 pounds off the scale by the time you get home – you figure around 6 pounds of baby, a couple pounds of blood and gunk, some serious ounces of fluid – you're 10 pounds closer to your goal weight! Yay! Way to go! Learn to celebrate the small victories ladies because you're gonna need them!

Especially if you're breastfeeding, the extra weight is not going to melt off your frame. You are on limited movement/exercise after birth, you have to eat to maintain nutrition/caloric needs for the baby, etc. Not to mention you have out of control hormones that can take months to settle down – and which of course, affect your ability to lose weight.

So time and small victories will be your friends. Be patient – you took 9 months to adjust your body to the pregnancy, so give yourself time to get it back to normal. Look into programs that might be available, talk to your physician, and know that you are always beautiful – because you are a mother!

We have both had miscarriages – unfortunately, it is a very common occurrence at various stages in pregnancy and it's possible that you might have to face this tragedy. There is a risk of miscarriage for every pregnancy, from anywhere to 10 to 25% of all pregnancies ending in miscarriage (first 20 weeks of gestation). Most miscarriages will occur in the first 13 weeks of gestation. Causes of miscarriage are as varied as their likelihood from mother to mother. Most are caused by chromosomal abnormalities – meaning that there is NOTHING you did wrong, there was something wrong and not viable about the baby's chromosomes such as a damaged egg or sperm or a problem during the division process for the zygote. THERE IS NOTHING YOU DID WRONG. There is nothing that says you won't go on to have five healthy babies. Unfortunately, there's nothing that says you won't have more than one miscarriage too. It is why mothers carry a badge of courage for what we are willing to endure to create and carry life.

Other causes for miscarriage may include, but are not limited to (nor are these absolute causes of miscarriage): hormonal problems, infections or maternal health problems, lifestyle choices (such as smoking, drinking, drug use, poor nutrition, excessive caffeine, exposure to toxic substances, etc…), implantation of the egg doesn't occur properly, the mother's age (if you're over 35, welcome to the world of Advanced Maternal Age), or trauma to the mother during pregnancy.

When you're pregnant, you may experience some spotting – the joy of pregnancy is that you will CONSTANTLY wonder if what you're experience is normal or if it's a sign of miscarriage. Sometimes, you will have zero signs of miscarriage (Amanda's case) and sometimes you'll have cramping with blood flow or anything in between. Pregnancy is that time in your life when if you're not sure, CALL YOUR DOCTOR. Every time. Better safe than sorry, which is why

Amanda got to know the ER very well in both her pregnancies – she was high risk and took no chances. Wasn't feeling the baby much? ER. Blood Pressure too high? ER. Leaking (turned out to be an infection), ER. See the pattern?

If you experience any or all of these symptoms, please call your doctor IMMEDIATELY if you have any cause for concern:

- Mild to severe back pain (often worse than normal menstrual cramps)
- Weight loss
- White-pink mucus
- True contractions (very painful happening every 5-20 minutes)
- Brown or bright red bleeding with or without cramps (20-30% of all pregnancies can experience some bleeding in early pregnancy, with about 50% of those resulting in normal pregnancies)
- Tissue with clot like material passing from the vagina
- Sudden decrease in signs of pregnancy

You're going to look for it anyways, so here's one of the most commonly referenced time tables for risk of miscarriage as your pregnancy progresses.

Gestational week (completed)	All healthy women	Healthy women, one live embryo seen on ultrasound
	% risk of miscarriage	% risk of miscarriage
3-4 weeks	22-75%	n/a
5-8 weeks	10%	n/a
6 weeks	n/a	9.4%
7 weeks	n/a	4.2%
8 weeks	n/a	1.5%
9 weeks	n/a	0.5%
10 weeks	n/a	0.7%
8-14 weeks	5%	n/a
2nd trimester	3%	n/a
3rd trimester	1%	n/a

References: Tong S, Kaur A, Walker SP, Bryant V, Onwude JL, Permezel M. Miscarriage risk for asymptomatic women after a normal first-trimester prenatal visit. Obstet Gynecol. 2008 Mar;111(3):710-4.
Wilcox AJ, Weinberg CR, O'Connor JF, et al. Incidence of early loss of pregnancy. N Engl J Med. Jul 28 1988;319(4):189-94.
http://pregnancyloss.info/statistics/

We've already told you that most miscarriages are due to chromosomes and that they are NOT your fault nor is there anything you could have done to prevent it. That being said, being as healthy as possible BEFORE conception and DURING pregnancy is critical to increasing your odds of carrying a healthy baby to term. So that being said, before you get pregnant, consider:

- Exercise regularly
- Eat healthy
- Manage stress
- Keep weight within healthy limits
- Take folic acid daily
- Do not smoke

Once you find out you're pregnant, (and really, if you're trying to conceive, you should kind of being doing most if not all of these anyways), provide a healthy body for your baby to grow in and:

- Keep your abdomen safe
- Do not smoke or be around smoke
- Do not drink alcohol
- Check with your doctor before taking any over-the-counter medications
- Limit or eliminate caffeine
- Avoid environmental hazards such as radiation, infectious disease and x-rays
- Avoid contact sports or activities that have risk of injury

Please allow your body time to heal and properly prepare for another try at pregnancy.

Chapter 18: SIDS (Sudden Infant Death Syndrome)

Knock on wood, neither of us has any experience with SIDS
(Sudden Infant Death Syndrome). You think your worries end when
you deliver your child? They are just beginning. Besides the every-
day worry of something, anything, happening to your child (which
may continue for the rest of their lives) there's the risk of SIDS.
Again, it's one of those things that the professionals are not able to
pinpoint an absolute cause of but they can provide a slew of things
you can do to MINIMIZE the risk of SIDS taking your baby from
you.

SIDS is the leading cause of death among 1 month to 1 year olds.
SIDS is the reason that you will freak out and go running into the
baby's room the first time he sleeps through the night. SIDS is the
reason you will stare at the baby monitor video to see the baby's
chest move as they breathe. It claims about 2,500 lives a year in the
U.S. and there are many things you can do to minimize the risk of it
happening to your child. But again, we have to stress, it is one of
those terrible, unfortunate, incomprehensible things that CAN
happen and we feel we HAVE to make sure you are aware and take
the steps necessary to try to prevent it from happening if at all
possible.

Remember that list of what to do to reduce your risk of miscarriage
during pregnancy? A lot of those apply here. Get good prenatal care
during your pregnancy. No drugs, no smoking, no drinking. SIDS is
linked to teenage pregnancies as well, perhaps going back to those
other factors. AFTER your baby is born, please, PLEASE, follow as
many if not all of these recommendations:

1. While Room-sharing is acceptable, bed-sharing is not
    recommended. If you are breastfeeding, it is recommended
    that you return the baby to his crib before you go back to

sleep to avoid accidental suffocation (rolling over onto the baby) or smothering.

2. Do not allow the baby to sleep with other children.
3. Use a bare crib mattress with a fitted sheet. Put nothing in the bed with the baby – no pillows, blankets, toys, positioning devices or covers. Remove the crib bumper. You want to make sure nothing can obstruct the baby's breathing or get close to her face.
4. Consider keeping the crib in the parents' room until the baby is able to easily roll from his back to his belly, and then to his back again from the belly position.
5. Babies with colds are at greater risk for SIDS.
6. Do not allow anyone to smoke around the baby. Do not have the baby in a room or vehicle where people are or have been smoking.
7. Offer your baby a pacifier (if breastfeeding, wait until the baby has successfully learned to latch on). Do not attach the pacifier to a sleeping baby as it can be a choking hazard.
8. Breastfeeding has been found in some studies to help reduce the risk of SIDS.
9. Give your baby plenty of tummy time on a play mat on the floor, not in bed where they may fall asleep face-down.
10. Do not put too many clothes on the baby or keep her room too warm/hot. If the baby is sweating, she is too warm.
11. If your baby gags excessively or stops breathing after spitting up, call your pediatrician IMMEDIATELY.
12. Review this list with all caregivers!

http://www.cdc.gov/sids/

http://www.babycenter.com/baby-sleep-safety

http://sids.org/

Contemplating Another Child?

Is it insanity? Totally. Should you do it? Absolutely!

'Nuff Said.

APPENDIX

Having gone through a few pregnancies and now raising five girls between us, Kim and I are the queens of consulting the internet and the "experts" on all kinds of topics addressed in this book, as well as inserting our personal opinions.

We do not claim to be medical experts, nor was this book written to be all-inclusive from a medical perspective. We take a real-life approach at explaining to you what may occur during average pregnancies and average deliveries. Your doctor is your expert, as is your body. Listen to them for all important guidance, look to us for real-world experience.

Nothing in this book was ripped directly from any one site except for the miscarriage table which is duly cited. We did want to provide some sites that we consider indispensible for child-rearing in case you are in your first pregnancy and want more information than you can possibly digest.

Smartphone App's
BabyCenter – Doug and I used it to record bottle feedings which helped me schedule the girls, plus it has all their vital information/growth stats in it. You can share the app between users so it's always up to date.

OurGroceries – you will eventually reach a point where you have to entrust the grocery shopping to your husband. This is another shared app where you can create all kinds of lists of items, and can even snap a picture of it or scan a UPC code so he can't possibly screw up the purchase. Yes, Doug has even purchased tampons for me. That's the sign of true love.

WhatToExpect – both for pregnancy and for baby's development once she arrives. It's just a nice "hey, here's what that pea pod is growing into and doing" inside your belly and a great "hey, your kid is 6 months old – have you started him on food yet?" kind of app. Non-invasive and a nice quick reference when you want it.

Websites

http://2mamabears.com Of course we're putting our associated site first! When you need some humor to go along with that advice….

http://www.babycenter.com very informative with a lot of different forums and information

http://www.whattoexpect.com based on the book that you will likely purchase or be given, it's a good source for additional information

http://www.thebump.com this is a really cute site that is full of forums, other women like you and all kinds of cutsie things

http://babyandbump.momtastic.com/ great for when you're trying to conceive as well as during your pregnancy.

http://www.fitpregnancy.com keep your weight gain to a minimum and you can avoid some issues during pregnancy

http://www.healthychildren.org/English/Pages/default.aspx Maintained by the American Academy of Pediatrics

38317670R00057

Made in the USA
Charleston, SC
04 February 2015